Jessie

with love

from Henning


April 1993

# Education for Special Needs

# Education for Special Needs

## Principles and Practice in Camphill Schools

Henning Hansmann

Floris Books

First published in English in 1992 by Floris Books.

British Library CIP Data available

ISBN 0-86315-138-8

Printed in Great Britain
by Dotesios Ltd, Trowbridge, Wilts.

# Contents

# Foreword

I consider it an honour and a privilege to be asked to write the foreword to *Education for Special Needs*. As a former employee of Grampian Regional Council, my working association with Camphill goes back over twenty years, but preparation for this book goes back much further, to the beginnings of the Camphill Movement in this country over fifty years ago. The book is a testimony to half a century of experience. The actual writing has taken somewhat less time, possibly five to eight years. While friends like myself have cajoled the author and tried to encourage earlier completion for publication, perhaps the pace of writing reflects the thoughtfulness and carefulness which typifies Camphill.

This book is a major presentation as Camphill enters the second half of its century. The list of contents may seem daunting at first glance. What is it about? It is a description of the life of the Community, the philosophy which is its bedrock, the class curriculum, the therapies, the totality of which provides "education for special needs." It tells us about the children and young people who are not "taken in" or "taken on" by the Community but who share and contribute to its life. This last statement is the core, namely that each child is special and each makes his unique contribution to the Community. It is this positive view, the respect for the individual, this philosophy which provides the energy, the patience and the love needed to help many of the children and young people achieve an inner peace and a better image of themselves. In Chapter 3 on "Education in the family group" there are many interesting illustrations of working with children and young people. These are presented positively. It is only in the incidental comment about some aspect of the young person's disruptive behaviour or in such statements as "this may take ten years to achieve" that one gets a glimpse of the extent of the underlying patience which enables the Community to care, to hold on and to support, sometimes beyond what might be expected humanly, and still deem that young person someone who has contributed to the life and growth of understanding of the Community: "Moments of crisis are often vital modes of growth in the nurturing of the child and this needs clear recognition and the loving courage to bear with him."

What is the source of this patience? Readers should be drawn to Chapter 2 on the philosophy which is the motivating force of the Community. Whatever one's own beliefs, there are so many meeting points, so many statements to which one nods in agreement. One can respect and trust without necessarily incorporating that philosophy personally. Trying to understand is a good starting point.

Chapter 4 on the principles of learning, based on an holistic view of child development, will be of particular interest to educationalists. The emphasis of the importance of the early years in learning and the value of play; the explanation of why certain stories are related at certain ages; of when and why certain subjects are introduced will be of much interest. How do they equate with the curriculum in State Schools for example? The block learning, the rhythm of teaching and memory all should give rise to thought and discussion. The follow-up description of "A year in the life of..." gives a further illustration of the class curriculum. There are some controversial statements regarding curriculum, pace of learning, grouping of handicap, but I will leave the reader to his own selection.

Throughout the book the importance of working with parents is stressed:

> When we admit a child in the Schools we become participants in the developmental process and in the interaction between the child and his parents. One of our first tasks is to listen to the parents and share their love for their child as well as their concern and despair. Few are likely to know more about a child than that child's mother and she is in the best position to provide observations of early childhood.

This theme of "sharing," of providing regular support for the family, being in regular communication and of making them welcome in the Community permeates the book.

*Education for Special Needs* has much information on the medical services provided including the various therapies, the continuous assessment process, the regular clinics and the College Meeting. This "multidisciplinary gathering is a convocation which focuses exclusively on one particular child." The reader should be in no doubt that while love, care and concern for the dignity of the child is paramount, the administrative organization of Camphill is thorough, efficient, comprehensive and ongoing. The College Meeting, however, will be mindful that "the true leader and teacher of the evening is the chosen child himself though not outwardly."

There is so much in this book. The life of the Community is before you whether you seek information about the Community itself, the understanding of its philosophy, the educational principles and practices or the variety of therapies which Camphill offers.

Many times over the years I have said to workers at the end of term when the children and young people go home for holidays: "You will be looking forward to some peace and quiet." Without exception the response, from the young seminarist to the experienced houseparent, has been the same: "Oh no, it is so empty without them. They are part of the life of our community." For many parents, at times burdened by having a child with a handicap and who have felt rejected by society, this book on *Education for Special Needs* in Camphill gives and lives a heartwarming message.

Margaret Taylor
*Former Principal*
*Educational Psychologist,*
*Grampian Region*

# Acknowledgments

This book is addressed to parents, professionals and all interested in children and young people who have special needs. My colleagues and I wish to share our experience and offer help towards understanding these children and their families. Our understanding and practice are inspired by the work of Rudolf Steiner and the founder of Camphill, Karl König.

We ask the reader to bear in mind that education for special needs (also known as "curative education") is one branch of the wider Waldorf education movement, founded by Rudolf Steiner. This is currently the largest independent school movement in the world, offering a comprehensive education to all children, with over five hundred schools worldwide.

The breath of the Camphill Community permeates everything presented here. Our gratitude and thanks go to the many children, their parents, our co-workers and other professionals who gave life and substance to the content of this book. Only a few can be mentioned by name for their untiring help towards the text: our consultants Douglas Haldane and Margaret Taylor; my colleagues Jens Holbek, Norma Lindenberg, Friedwart and Nora Bock, Peter Hansmann and, not least, our secretaries, Nan Wright and Liz Mackie. Contributors to the chapter on medical and therapeutic care were: Nicolas Blitz, Annelies Bruell, Bernd Ehlen, Mali Evans, the late Trude Gross, Maria Halder, Sigrid Hansmann, Christine Holbek, Robert Liddiard, Julian Marx, David Newbatt, Russ Pooler and Joseph Shacher. Thanks are also due to Paul Bock for the use of his fine photographs.

The names of the children have been altered throughout. The personal pronoun "he" has been used for children, and "she" for educators, of both genders, as this relates to the actual proportion of male and female pupils and co-workers.

Work on this book was started whilst I was one of three Principals of the Camphill–Rudolf–Steiner–Schools. Meanwhile, these responsibilities have been passed on to others.

Henning Hansmann
Christmas 1991

# 1 An introduction to Camphill

Only help from man to man, the encounter of Ego with Ego —
the awareness of the other man's individuality — without
inquiring into his creed or his world concept or his political
affiliations, but simply the meeting, I to I of two individualities
— only this creates the kind of curative education which may
counter and heal the threat to the inner man.

These words of Karl König (1902–65), founder of the Camphill Rudolf
Steiner Schools at Aberdeen and the worldwide Camphill Movement, are
a directive to Camphill's work and life.[1] The word "Ego," in our context,
means: the spiritual part of our human existence which does not belong
to space and time. The Ego was before we were born and will be after
we have died, and while we are on Earth it works, develops and gathers
experience through our personality which is always bound to earthly
limitations. This idea can lead to an understanding of reincarnation about
which more will be said later. The term "curative education" refers to the
education of children and adolescents with special needs due to mental,
emotional and/or physical handicaps. It will be explained further in the
last part of this chapter.

Dr Karl König and his wife, Tilla (1901–83), founded our Schools at
Aberdeen in 1940 together with a small group of refugees from Austria
— among them Dr Thomas Weihs (1914–83), and his wife Anke Weihs
(1914–87), the Reverend Peter Roth, who became the founder of the
Camphill Village Trust, his sister Alix Roth (1916–87), and Carlo Pietzner (1915–86), who later founded Camphill's work in the USA. Today,
1991, this Movement comprises over eighty communities in fifteen
countries.[2] It is part of the wider Rudolf Steiner Movement of Curative
Education and Social Therapy.

# Pupils, resources and curriculum

Our resources here at Aberdeen are similar to those of other Camphill Schools for children and young people with special needs, and the ideas and ideals of our curriculum and of living in community are the same. The descriptions and philosophy presented here can, therefore, be seen as relevant to all schools in the Camphill Movement, though there are, of course, local variations and some schools are much smaller.

The pupils attending our Schools suffer from disorders including emotional and behavioural disturbances, autism, epilepsy and mental retardation, cerebral palsy, deafness and blindness. Many of the pupils suffer from more than one of these impairments. In our experience, children and young people with such special needs develop better if they are not segregated according to their diagnostic types; in sharing life with others who have different abilities and impairments they, and all of us who live and work here, complement and help one another so that what was handicap can become potential.

Pupils are referred to the Schools by Education and Social Services departments of local authorities throughout the United Kingdom. The child, the parents and others concerned are interviewed by our Medical Officer and if it is considered that the child can benefit from attending our Schools, his name is placed on the waiting list until a suitable vacancy occurs in a family unit as well as in the appropriate School class. We give preference to children whose situations require urgent action, either because of their own stress or stress in the family. The final decision about admission is made by the houseparents and the teacher into whose care and guidance the child will be placed. The children and young people who come to our Schools need the concern and guidance of a coherent community which provides a total educational environment.

Our Schools are located on three estates totalling 135 acres in the Dee Valley within the boundaries of the city of Aberdeen. In addition to the three original mansion houses, which have been extensively modified, there are thirteen purpose-built units, each housing from eight to thirty-five souls, staff and their families together with the pupils. Five school buildings are located on these estates. There are also nursery school facilities, a gymnasium, a swimming pool, special therapy rooms and an indoor riding school. Camphill Hall is a large, beautiful assembly hall

*Classrooms and the swimming pool at the Camphill Schools*

with stage and chapel, constantly used. Two assembly rooms, craft teaching workshops, two joinery production workshops, a purpose–built G.P. surgery, a medical dispensary and a sick–bay also form part of the complex. Each estate has a sizeable, organically–run vegetable garden and there is a smallholding with some stock. The rural environment of the estates provides rich opportunity for play and leisure activity while the proximity of Aberdeen allows for social contact and integration, such as work experience placement and visits to the theatre, cinema, concerts or other cultural events.

The staff and their families share life with our pupils as their natural parents would do at home. They are not on or off duty but are available at all times. Each has, of course, his special field of work as houseparent, teacher, therapist, nurse, craftsman, gardener or doctor, but everyone shares in the practical work which daily life at home requires. Each dwelling unit is the overall responsibility of experienced houseparents who are supported by other senior staff and the group–parents (who care for two to four pupils), all ideally living under the same roof. The pupils in the house vary in age and have different impairments while each group comprises pupils of the same sex and similar age. Each household caters and cooks for itself and staff, their families and the pupils share their meals. In this way pupils come to regard this place as their home and learn to participate in the care of the house and the estate. As they mature they develop a sense of responsibility to one another as well as for the upkeep of the fabric and the land.

The acceptance of the child and young person who has a handicap and/or an emotional disturbance as a developing individual in the community is a keystone of our work. We endeavour to meet his needs with a curriculum which embraces the whole twenty–four hours of the day and all seven days of a week. The rhythms of learning and relaxing, of work and play, of weekday and Sunday, of term time and holidays are essential to this. In many of our pupils the natural rhythms of breathing, sleeping and waking, eating and digesting, remembering and forgetting are disturbed and can be newly established through the rhythms of life in home and classroom. The curriculum offers rich opportunities for incidental and tacit learning and, as the pupil grows older, consciously–directed and functional learning are increasingly fostered. Both aspects are valid in the classroom as well as in home life and leisure time.

The eighteen classes vary in number from five to sixteen children. The pupils are taught by their class teacher with the help of two or more

assistants, special subject teachers, and in some circumstances, of therapists. They attend classes, from nursery class upwards, according to their
chronological age, and the syllabus is based on a developmental approach
to learning. In the first part of the morning the teacher and assistants
work with the whole class together. In breaktime the children are guided
in play and organized games. Afterwards, the pupils reassemble in small
groups, or for individual work under the guidance of the class teacher,
therapists and assistants when each pupil's individual learning problems
can be assessed and aided. In the afternoons pupils have lessons in arts
and crafts and the older ones may have placements in workshops and
gardens to gain practical skills.

A three–year Upper School course for sixteen– to nineteen–year–olds
includes training and work experience. Further education courses for
young adults from sixteen or eighteen upwards are also conducted at
other Camphill Communities in Britain to which senior pupils may
transfer, the nearest being a horticulturally based community, Beanna-
char, south of the Dee. We also have a community home, Tigh a' Cho-
mainn, at Peterculter in Aberdeen, for young adults who still wish to
have our support but are independent enough to go out on their own for
training and work.

Back to the curriculum, it places considerable emphasis on creating a
cultural life with the pupils who join in the production of concerts and
plays. Highlights for these are the seasonal festivals which we celebrate
together. We also hold non–denominational Christian Sunday Services.
At the end of a term a "School Festival" takes place in our beautiful
Hall, during which classes present some of their work as plays and
music, songs and poems or a part of a lesson to the entire Schools'
community. These festivals provide us all with a good opportunity to see
individual children's progress and the development of each class, often
a moving experience. Parents and friends are warmly encouraged to
participate in these events.

Holidays are an essential part of life's curriculum, needed for the
pupils' maturation and, where possible, the reintegration into the young
person's home and the wider community. The breathing between holidays
spent at home and term time at school is of intrinsic value. The holiday
periods are approximately three weeks after Christmas and Easter and in
October, and five weeks in summer, so that most children are with us for
thirty–eight weeks in the year. Exceptions are made when help is needed
during holidays.

The healing work of Camphill is surrounded by an "outer skin" which serves mutual concerns, communication and protection. This is formed by a national parents' association with regional parents links — more will be said later about our work with parents — and by the councils of our two charitable companies; one is the legal owner of the Schools' property and cares about capital and development, and the other has the legal responsibility for revenue and the general running of the Schools. Camphill could not exist without the support and friendship of parents and locally well-known respected personalities who serve as honorary directors.

# Organization

The central responsibility for the life community of the Schools is carried by the "Camphill Meeting" to which every staff member may belong. The spirit of the meeting is best expressed in Rudolf Steiner's motto for social ethics (which he gave to Edith Maryon):

> Healing comes only
> when in the mirror of the Human Soul
> the whole Community is formed
> and when in the Community
> the virtue of the Individual One is effective.

Together with and on behalf of the Camphill Meeting a fair number of professional and administrative groups and committees is needed to guide the "ship" forward and through all weathers.

Our educational work is embedded in the triad of home life, school and therapies, these are the domains of three professional groups: the Houseparents (responsible for all aspects of life in our family units), the College of Teachers, and the College of Therapists. They in turn work together with our resident doctors, nurses and our consultants. Mutual support of their members, conducting of continuous staff training and self assessment, organizing conferences and training students are essential parts of their work. The areas of their responsibilities will be described further.

At the hub of the administration is the group of joint co-ordinators (previously principals group) who work together with committees which in turn have responsibilities for such concerns as: the admission of pupils; of staff, students and helpers; fees and finances; building, devel-opment and the land; public relations; also *ad hoc* groups concerned with the preparation of national and international conferences of which we may host two or three a year.

These groups are community forms which evolve and are flexible, their membership changes, but the spirit of social ethics referred to at the beginning of this chapter continues to give direction.

# Training in curative education

The term "curative education" is a translation of *Heilpädagogik,* a word commonly used in German speaking countries. Asperger wrote in 1956:

> Curative education is that science which, building on biologically
> founded knowledge of pathological personalities of children,
> seeks predominantly pedagogical means for the treatment of
> intellectual and sensory defects, of nervous and emotional
> disturbances in children and adolescents.

He described psychiatry, paediatrics, psychology, sociology and education as the "five head waters" of curative education.[3]

Sixteen years after founding the Course at Camphill inspired by anthroposophy, Karl König wrote that curative education:

> ...was and is a developing science which has a connection with
> child psychiatry and is aided by paediatrics, neurology and
> psychology. It is also a practical ever–unfolding art. It plays its
> part in pedagogics, special education, as well as in many other
> areas, like speech therapy, physiotherapy, eurythmy and curative
> eurythmy, painting, drawing, music and music therapy, also in
> handcrafts, such as weaving, pottery, wood–carving and occu-
> pational therapy. In its widest aspects curative education is not
> only science, not only practical art, but a *human attitude.* It can
> be administered like a healing medicine to the human individual
> who stands under the threat of being destroyed. This, however, is
> the destiny of every human being today. To counter this threat,
> to help and to receive help is the meaning and value of curative
> work.[4]

The philosophy and practice of curative education as described here place great responsibilities and demands on anyone who wishes to be–

come a curative educator. Therefore, in 1949, Karl König started "The Course in Curative Education" at Camphill, Aberdeen. It has become a wellspring of the Camphill Movement which by now has spread to fifteen countries. The Course has since been taken up by other Camphill centres in seven countries (see appendix). Today curative education, as practised in Camphill, is an art and a way of life which require continuing scientific research and training of practical skills. Three to four years plus a probationary period are usually needed for any student to learn the fundamentals of this art and discipline before she is ready to work independently and responsibly as a curative educator. The successful student can then be expected to know how to continue working on her personal development, also how to study and improve her methods together with her colleagues — a lifelong task. One of the maxims taught to students is that no child will make real progress unless his educator is prepared to make as much progress on her own path as she asks of the child. Original gifts, acquired skills and experience are very helpful but they do not replace this human attitude.

# 2 Philosophy and principles

## A day in the life of Paul

We shall begin by describing a day in the life of Paul, aged thirteen years, who shares a bedroom with three boys of his own age.

At 7 am he is woken by music sounding through the house, played perhaps on a flute. His group–father encourages him to face the day — to wash, to dress, make his bed and tidy up his belongings — before the gong sounds in time for morning assembly, when the household gathers in front of the dining–room, quietly waiting until the last straggler has arrived so that the door can be opened. A daily morning verse is spoken by all, or a text from the Gospels is read, and a seasonal morning song is sung before breakfast begins. Paul has been with us for several years and he has, therefore, been given a place next to Frankie, who, due to his spastic condition, is unable to feed himself. Food is one of Paul's great indulgences but, as he has to feed Frankie and prevent his hands from waving about, Paul's own intake remains within the desired limits. His self–centred, dreamy personality is awakened by the needs and smiles of his dependent neighbour. The meal is concluded, children and adults together clear the tables and now everyone has to be alert as there is not much time before going off to school. Everyone helps to the best of his ability, to put the house in order. Some beds have yet to be made, rooms swept, dead flowers replaced. Paul puts on his apron and begins to wash the dishes with a vengeance, totally oblivious of the fact that his helpers are not there; then, suddenly waking up from his preoccupation with his own job, exclaims miserably: "Why has nobody come to help!?" They do come and help and Paul completes his job well on time. Perhaps there will still be time to feed the cat and play his daily

exercise on his recorder, but by 9 am he will have to be in his classroom.

Paul has come a long way since he first arrived at school as a "bouncing ball" of undirected energy, dropping from his chair every few
minutes and rolling along the floor in fits of uncontrollable giggling.
Incessant movement and obsessional preoccupations have given way to
gradual awareness of the school situation and the presence of other
children and his teacher. "Should we love the mole?" he once asked with
genuine puzzlement in a block period on "Man and Animal," a first
indication of active involvement in an issue of "moral" value. From then
on islands of understanding have begun to form. Now his interest is
aroused most readily by demonstrations in physics or chemistry but he
has also become aware of the interrelation of Man and nature and of
Man's dependence on his fellows, through subjects such as geography.
Paul needs a long time to "grow" into a subject and it is fortunate that
the long daily geography lesson is continued over several weeks so that
the life of the Red Indian or the Eskimo can begin to become an experience to him, especially when drama, painting and drawing are used as an
expression of what he is being taught. After the mid–morning break Paul
spends the last hour before lunch at reading and arithmetic. He has
acquired some mechanical skill but lacks comprehension and his active
interest in the subject needs to be aroused from minute to minute; a
strenuous process for Paul and teacher alike.

By 12.30 morning school is over and Paul is encouraged to assist his
room–mate, Tony, whose extreme fastidiousness about his looks frequently prevents him from arriving at lunch on time — never a problem for
hungry Paul. The midday meal needs time. After grace the dishes are
passed around and Paul has learned to leave a sufficient amount of meat
in the dish, to allow others their share. Some eat slowly, some rapidly;
— Frankie may spill his water — but we all finish together at about a
quarter to two. After Paul has helped Frankie to climb up the stairs to his
room he will give a hand in the kitchen and, with his group–father, discuss plans for his free time until afternoon lessons begin. Whereas the
frailer and smaller children will have a rest on their beds, perhaps with
a favourite toy or a book, Paul may be doing his homework, practising
the recorder or playing a game, taking some articles to the dry cleaner
in the local suburb, cycling around the estate or just dreaming away in
the sunshine on a bench in the garden. His fantasy is wild and morbid,
filled with images of his heroes from the TV screen and so care is given

that the books he reads, or leafs through, are of some artistic merit and content.

Just before 3 pm Paul needs a reminder from his group–father not to miss his woodwork lesson where his confrontation with a large piece of wood, to be shaped into a beautifully smooth bowl for his mother, is of therapeutic value. And then — the first rehearsal for the King Arthur Pageant, to be performed at Whitsun. Paul jumps about excitedly, hands flapping, his face lit up with a wide smile. Will he be allowed to participate as a knight this year or only as a mere squire? At the Easter celebration he had no special part, but the songs, the music, the egg-painting, the plays, the sowing and planting on Good Friday all filled his hungry soul with meaningful food and he has been enquiring over and over again about the next event. And now the long struggle towards expressive speech and gesturing begins, tackled by Paul with near fana-tical perseverance. Those who watch him at the rehearsals do not know that at the performance Paul, whom some would call autistic, will later move some of the audience near to tears by the intense goodwill and longing for recognition of his true person which shines through the simple words of the knightly vows. The rehearsal is over, perhaps there is still time for a swim, but Paul is eager to know what supper will bring. After supper a verse is spoken which, together with a song, will conclude the day for everyone and, while the youngest children go to bed, Paul will still spend some time playing games outside, watering the garden or perhaps working on his model plane with his group–father. Paul is tired, for he has had a full day, a day filled with work, relax-ation, social involvement and artistic expression. By nine o'clock he and his room–mates will be in bed, enjoying another chapter of the book read by his group–father and, if time permits, a quiet talk followed by prayer.

Paul's day is only part of a week, a year, which we try to structure so that there can be meaning to the pattern of our lives — year after year attempting to grow towards an understanding of the interplay between human being and nature, the seasons and their vital landmarks, the Christian festivals. It is through Paul's participation in this process that some of his anxieties and tensions may be alleviated and that acceptance of his destiny as a person with special needs and courage for the future, can grow in him. Paul is gathering strength — strength to face his limi-tations, to carry his burden by recognizing values that lie hidden behind outer appearance. Carrying the weight of this burden can lead to maturity through which Paul will be able to find his way. However limited his ultimate contribution may be, we hope to have led him to the experience of his own humanity, which only he, as a unique individual, can offer to the world.

# An holistic philosophy

Our work at Camphill is based on anthroposophy, which was first evolved by Rudolf Steiner (1861–1925). He conceived anthroposophy as a new wisdom of the spiritual, mental and physical nature of Man; a wisdom which does not remain merely abstract knowledge but which kindles motivation and creativity. His teaching was influenced by the great Middle European thinkers and philosophers as well as by the contemporary developments in the natural sciences. Rudolf Steiner was one of those rare individuals who could embrace the knowledge of his time. He united this knowledge with his deep spiritual experience out of which his own teaching was born. Anthroposophy, as he taught it, is imbued with a Christian faith which is born out of spiritual perception. It opens up a new understanding of modern science as well as current social questions. It is also a wellspring for future developments of healing in medical and educational work, in agriculture and many other fields of human endeavour.[5]

We at Camphill work on the basis of anthroposophy, but not only for those who are connected with anthroposophy or anthroposophical work. We work for the world endeavouring to meet needs of our time and to uphold human values. We want to serve the true "Image of Man" wherever it is threatened and in danger of being distorted. We see an image of Man, the image of God, as a divine ideal which lives in every human being, however much he falls short of it. An artist who creates an image expands part of his being into it so that it may speak through the material which he uses. In Genesis it says: "Let us make man in our image according to our likeness." We hold that this image of Man is the greatest work of art in the world. The creator has expanded his spirit into the image of Man and speaks through it so that he may come to live through the eye of the beholder. Therefore, we can recognize the divine spirit in every human being. Each one of us depends on others who may recognize the divine origin in ourselves. Increasing scientific knowledge about

*Human interaction is at the heart of all our activities*

hereditary factors transmitted by genes tells us about the material and techniques the Creator uses when fashioning the human form and therefore, makes it all the more clear that the image of Man, as it appears in the human form, is of a different order from the hereditary forces. The latter may be interfered with but we have no influence on the former.

When upholding the image of Man in every human encounter we do not primarily look for quantifiable success; what matters is the human effort and striving to create a better world. This effort is shared with those children and young people who are entrusted to us for an essential part of their lives; with the students whom we train in Curative Education and who give of their strength and their love to the work we are doing; with all the professionals who refer children to us and lastly, but by no means least, with the parents of the children and with friends who support our work. Our philosophy upholds the spiritual uniqueness with which each human being is endowed. The spiritual element of the human being is always whole and can never be impaired. We put our trust in the unique spirit which lives in each person, whatever his age, his gifts or impairments. We put our faith in the meaningfulness of his destiny even if we may not always understand it. His being may be hindered or trapped by impairments of his body and his environmental circumstances. The acceptance of impairments and hindrances as meaningful contains seeds of strength, needed to live with and, where possible overcome disability and suffering.

Concepts of normalization such as those arrived at by calculating statistical averages of isolated aspects of human development are not subscribed to by Rudolf Steiner education. The aim is to guide each child and young person through a process of individualization. In the initial acceptance and subsequent struggle with hindrances, the growing individual can gain strength and a meaningful place in his family and in the wider society. We have to give guidance and create space for this process and support each individual on his own path of development. The meaning of handicap and of social deprivation can never be grasped if our human existence is looked upon as being bounded by conception (or birth) and by death; nor can it be understood if a child is seen in isolation from the family into which he is born or those with whom he shares life. The child who is dear to us and about whom we despair because he has a handicap, because he is "different," can open doors for us which lead to a deeper understanding of ourselves, for in every handicap we may see a one–sided exaggeration of some aspect or quality which lives in each human being but which is usually kept in balance.

Thomas Weihs often spoke of this view of what are called handicaps. In March 1983, three months before his death, "Dr Thomas," as he was affectionately known to hosts of children, said to a gathering of parents of children and adults who are handicapped:

I should like to say something about the children, for and with whom we in the Camphill Communities have worked for so many years. In much they have been the teachers of their teachers, the therapists of their therapists. In their one-sidednesses, they have shown us the glory of the total human potential and they have given us the opportunity of helping others in a way that has helped us to develop our own integrity, maturity and fulfilment. They have been our support and our allies in all our tasks. The fantastic progress of modern science in many fields has not increased our happiness and sense of wellbeing nor our faith in the ultimate spirituality of the human being. It will be important for the future to create further communities based on the mutual recognition and help between the so-called normal and the so-called handicapped as a contribution to the social rejuvenation of the wider community.[6]

When meeting a child or young person who has a handicap, the age-old Gospel question is asked anew: Is it his fault or the fault of his parents or has he come to demonstrate the glory of God? (John 9). In modern terms we may ask, is his condition a consequence of his deeds in former lives on Earth or is it imposed on him by us, by our way of conducting our lives in the present time, or has he come to bring healing into our society and prepare our future on Earth? We know that every year a definite, even if small, number of children die or are severely damaged by vaccinations and through their sacrifice many others are protected from certain illnesses. We are aware that children who are born with Down's Syndrome bring a capacity of love and human interest into our time which far exceeds what is usual, but they are little concerned about intellectual achievement, money and sex. The so-called deprived and maladjusted child carries a particular burden which makes him test our truthfulness and highlights the brittleness of modern society.

We may ask: are those children merely "accidents" of our society, as some would have it, children who should not be allowed to live, or are they individuals who have been chosen to bring an offering in this life for the sake of all of us? Do they, through their very existence, form a host of the powerless who teach us about our past and help us to forge our future; who make us aware of reincarnation and the development of the human individual? We are bound to meet the consequences of our deeds done, or omitted in the past and, with everything we do in the present, we prepare our future. Even our thoughts and feelings are not solely "private"; they direct our own conduct and they influence those with whom we share life.

Rudolf Steiner spoke about reincarnation out of his own spiritual perception and experience. In this he shared his conviction with many major world religions other than Christianity and with many currently subordinated strands of Christian thought. The spiritual experience of our own human existence, before birth as well as after death, finds its reverberations and has become more known in Europe and in the Western World particularly since the middle of this century. It is no longer a premise of poets, but it is shared by an increasing number of children and young people. An enquiry into teenage religion by Harold Loukes has shown that the majority of senior school children in Britain think that they have lived on Earth in previous lives.[7] One young person is quoted as saying: "I think you kind of come back into the world again, to live and lead a better life, and you go on coming back until you're perfect, and then, well, there isn't a place, but I think you go to God when you're perfect." In a recent Gallup Poll it is stated that 27% of a cross-section of the population in England and Scotland believe in reincarnation and among young adults (16 to 24) it is 35%, and among women of all ages it is 32%.

Reincarnation, as Rudolf Steiner perceived it, is not a wheel of endless repetition; neither is it a process in which we try to free ourselves from all earthly burdens as was taught by certain Eastern religions. It is a path of development which leads the individual human spirit together with the whole of humankind through history as it evolves on Earth. This history involves not only us as human beings, who experience birth and death, but it is also part of the evolution of spirit beings who are far greater than we. Rudolf Steiner felt a deep commitment to open up an understanding of the experience of reincarnation for modern European and Western thinking and for scientific knowledge. He showed us that the magnificent discoveries of Charles Darwin and his contemporaries need not be seen as an indication that Man evolves from the animals. They can be understood as demonstrating that Man existed spiritually before the animals. Traces of human physical evolution found on the Earth show the stepping stones which were needed before the spiritual essence of Man could begin to incarnate into earthly existence.

The same holds good for the biogenetic law postulated by Haeckel that the ontogeny of the individual, which is the embryological development, is a repetition of the phylogeny of the species, the physical unfolding of the animal kingdom. In other words, in the time between conception and birth each human being goes through phases which repeat the necessary physical stepping stones of the incarnation of the human race on Earth and these phases are reminiscent of the evolution of the whole animal kingdom. When a child is born he continues to repeat early phases of the development of Man. These include the acquisition of uprightness, speech and the power of thinking which were bestowed on humankind by the divine powers which guide our lives.[8] The founder of the Camphill Movement, Karl König, who studied these three steps of child development in great depth said (in an unpublished lecture), it is easy to understand that there can be interruption and failure in the development of these faculties because it is such a delicate and highly complicated process: indeed it is a miracle that it usually succeeds.

In our first two to three years of life, which for most of us are not accessible to our memory, we learn far more than at any other time.[9] Conscious memories which we can distil out of our past, manifest but a small aspect of our life although they are important for our awareness of personal identity. The larger part of our experiences sooner or later sinks down below the threshold of our usual awareness into forgetting and there it contributes to the substance and colour of our character and individuality. Similarly, what we have experienced in the course of the evolution of humankind has become essence and substance of our spiritual self. We have participated in every epoch of history and its different modes of human consciousness. These have built up the faculties which we bring with us as our potential when entering a new life on Earth. The time between death and a new birth can be likened to a very long sleep which is needed to renew our strength, our love and our determination to live again. It takes a long time until a new epoch calls us and our contemporaries to share life on Earth anew.

It is implicit in our Christian faith to trust that the divine powers who guide human destiny, love Man. They give a measure of freedom to the individual and this commits him to the consequences of his deeds. As self-conscious human beings we are aware of this freedom but we

*Both confidence and joy come with achieving*

cannot fully know what the consequences of our deeds may be, neither are we fully aware of all the events in the past which have led up to the present circumstances. Powers far greater than our own are needed to weave the web of destiny into which a child is born and to guide onward what we should take with us when we die. We depend on their grace, yet we, with our measure of freedom, are involved in this process. When a child is to be born, his individual spiritual heritage, his gifts and talents have to unite with a stream of earthly, parental, hereditary forces. He has to find his parents through whom his physical body can be conceived, even if he cannot find the most perfect hereditary substance nor the ideal human environment. It is the spiritual element of the child that "chooses" parents, and the parents may accept or reject the child. It is the child who loves his parents first and it is up to the parents to respond to this. Whatever parents believe to have been their choice and their planning, does not alter the more profound truth that they are "chosen" by their child. Our knowledge of genetics and our powers of interference in the course of conception and birth, place responsibilities on us for which we are hardly ready. We live in a time of great confusion: this is not to decry our fate but rather to recognize our situation. Suffering and failure belong to the process of all learning and can help us to gain wisdom and increase our strength and loving concern.

# A total educational environment

An all-round education is the birthright of every child, regardless of handicap and intellectual ability. Some children's needs cannot adequately be met in their local school and in their home. This does not mean that their parents or school are to blame for their condition but some children cannot cope with the everyday demands of their environment. A child suffering from autism might not cope with the frustration he causes his loving and devoted parents because he cannot readily respond to them and often seems to reject them. An adolescent, deprived of parental love at an early age, might be unable to conduct himself in a socially acceptable manner. A child who is too restless and demanding at home, or too slow and unable to keep up with others, may become deeply frustrated because he cannot make that contribution to his environment which would allow his true individuality to shine forth.

The Camphill Community has, since its inception in 1940, endeavoured to provide an environment in which an all–round education can be offered. It is not a Community *for* children; it is a Community *with* children. In their "house communities," children and adults learn to know each other intimately. They share in joy and sorrow, each has something to give and each can mutually learn from the other; a discipline which needs to be learned and requires continuous self–education. The adults strive to set an example which can kindle a spark of self–education in each child and becomes a little flame in him by the time he is an adolescent who wants to leave school. This can then be nurtured by his own growing motivation towards goodness, towards wanting to care about and give something to his fellow men. In our life, education starts in the morning when the child is woken, continues throughout the day and it does not end when he is settled for the night. Children also need to be accompanied in their sleep by our awareness and good thoughts. We strive to form a ring around our pupils, which is forged from loving awareness and understanding.

Our Community can never be static, because the continuous flow of new pupils, student co–workers and helpers carries with it the waves of new development. The interaction with parents and professionals keeps us in direct contact with every aspect of society. This spurs us to meet the challenges of the present time and search for the meaning and purpose of our lives. The children who come to us reflect problems current in our society. The child found as a babe in a bag, dumped in a dustbin, and the child from a well–protected, caring family–background may become playmates here.

In the 1960's we experienced a wave of children suffering from autism. In the 1970's, large numbers of emotionally disturbed and/or socially deprived children came to us. The early 1980's brought a rising number of children suffering from schizophrenic breakdowns and the later 1980's children and teenagers who act out their frustration in violence. They all challenge us to deepen our understanding of the present time and to guide them towards integration into the wider community without allowing their pathology to dominate.

This total educational environment is not an aim in itself. Most pupils and staff children who have grown up here have developed "an understanding of the heart" for handicap and suffering (their own and others'); they have gained in human dignity. When our pupils leave, although they may well be a little reticent, they have something to give to society.

There are, inevitably, also some who cannot socially integrate anywhere and lead a tragic life. Others who had to experience time in prison, can later on, perhaps when they are over twenty–five, make good use of the values they have absorbed here and then go on to lead a life which is satisfying to them. We feel however, that we may not judge them according to their ability to fit in with society. Some who may have changed little can cope with life and others who have made great progress by virtue of their own efforts may still fall foul of the law, commit suicide, feel unfulfilled — and be considered as inadequate. However, some of them have also made a deep impression on the social conscience of their fellow human beings.

# Human relationships and social education

## *Parents and family*

Parents represent the ultimate source of security in the life of a child, so mutual confidence and trust between the parents and ourselves is essential to help the progress of our pupils. The drama of physical birth is only the beginning of a process which takes the child some twenty years to make the transition into adulthood. Mother and father provide much more than a physical shelter for the child; mother especially, whose way of being and living provides that necessary enveloping "skin" for her child in its early years. A second "birth" of a different order takes place when the child is ready to cast off this invisible "skin" of early childhood and enter school but he still depends on home as the "nest" to which he can return every day. On reaching adolescence he must discard another part of the childhood protection, up to this moment provided by his parents. At this point he sets out to meet his personal destiny and he wants to be "different" from his parents; yet, invisible bonds remain to give so much joy and pain to the adolescent and his parents. These are very real and necessary supports for the young person if he is to achieve true independence and for the parents if they are to set him free. Adulthood is achieved when the last part of this invisible "skin" has been laid aside and the young person is freed to forge his own destiny. A fresh bond of mutual love can then develop between parents and their now adult son or daughter.

When we admit a child to the Schools we become participants in this developmental process and in the interaction between the child and his parents. One of our first tasks is to listen to the parents and share their love for their child as well as their concern and despair. Few are likely to know more about a child than that child's mother and she is in the best position to provide observations of early childhood. Good contact with the parents allows them to continue to feel involved in the development of their child while he is with us. In this way mutual understanding is fostered and our efforts to guide their child — even though our ways of doing this may be different from theirs — can support and complement each other. We keep in close contact with parents by telephone and letter and by sending them the same detailed annual reports about their children as are sent to the local authority concerned. Contact can be easier when parents live nearby but it does not depend on distance alone. Many parents accept our invitations to come, sometimes from considerable distance, and join us for our various seasonal and school festivals. It is most rewarding to experience the joy and interaction between them and their children on such occasions.

Holidays are important stepping stones for the child's development and maturation. A child attending a boarding school needs to have a home outside the school environment. Life at school is devoted to education and upbringing, but a child's home is part of that world, often harsh, which he may want to rejoin when he leaves school behind. His image and experience of the world into which he then re–enters are strongly determined by the parental home and its environment. Moreover, parents themselves need to "grow up" with their children and, for this, a family needs to spend sufficient time together. If all goes well it is a process of mutual maturation: the child entering into life, the parents growing in wisdom and experience, all having much to give to each other. As educators we try to support this process, aware of the pain and injury it can cause if, for one reason or another, this mutual growth and development is disturbed, interrupted or even destroyed. For those children who are rejected at home or have no parents, we relate to their social workers and, if appropriate, the children might spend their holidays with foster parents or in children's homes. Sometimes foster parents can successfully do as actual parents should do. In exceptional circumstances our community might provide holidays for them, but original unconditional parental love cannot be replaced by good ideas, not even by goodwill.

Education always means preparing the future and from the start we must think ahead together with the parents. They may, and most usually do, feel deeply attached to their child but his special needs may put their love to the test when he reaches adolescence and perhaps presents new and sometimes quite serious difficulties. We endeavour to prepare parents and make them aware of the various stages of development. There are bound to be times of crisis which may cause behaviour problems, there may be illness or even accidents. At such moments parents will be included and may be asked to visit: moments of crisis are often vital nodes of growth in the maturing of their child and this needs clear recognition and the loving courage to bear with him.

It is necessary that the parents and we work together to prepare their child and themselves for the time of school–leaving and, where possible, reintegration into the social environment at home. Every school leaver is bound to have illusions about himself and his future life but as a rule he has the strength to learn by experience and eventually establish himself as an adult in his own right. For the young person who has special limitations because of his handicaps this requires more preparation, care and support than usual. He needs both his parents and our help to develop a realistic picture of his future after leaving school. If this cannot be given he is in danger of deteriorating or breaking down. At sixteen a period of extended schooling with further education and training may be indicated, and this can be all the more successful when it has the whole-hearted support of parents. Young people, however handicapped they might be, wish to make up their own minds but they do accept guidance when parents, teachers and other adults concerned are united in the advice and support which they offer. Much tact is required in approaching these matters at the right time. There is a great sense of achievement and joy in a young adult who, after a long struggle, has come to terms with a childhood handicap and can return to his family, to spend some time at home. Then, if in the course of time, home turns out no longer to be the right place for him, he and his parents can have a new and free relationship which will accompany him in his adult life. We often have visits of former pupils, some may bring their ageing parents along. Such visits are a source of warmth and reassurance.

## The community and the spiritual family

The transition from the time–honoured traditional family structure to a future which calls for individual responsibility, is a struggle in which we are all involved. Today, structures have to be created newly by the individuals as tradition alone can no longer provide a socially viable setting. At the beginning of the last century only about fifty percent of the population was likely to marry but a family was, then, a large social and economic unit. Grandparents, aunts, uncles, nephews and nieces were part of such a family and it might include apprentices, servants and their relatives. Often there were eight, twelve or more children, many of whom died in early infancy or childhood. Today, over ninety–five percent of the population marry, yet there is a steep increase in the incidence of divorce and re–marriage. A family with three children is nowadays found to be large; one speaks of "one–parent families," and there are many.

In 1902, the Swedish writer Ellen Kay called our century the "Century of the Child," an expression of a new conscience speaking within the modern human being. Every helpless new–born child arrives with complete trust and openness and can replenish the emptying vessels of our confidence in destiny and ourselves. He also offers a challenge to our humanity and goodwill. Mother finds that she is to open up the world of her child's senses and father may have each day to decide that he will be an example to his child. Of course both parents can share either aspect because there are motherly and fatherly elements in each of us. Today, the living reality of any family depends on the two individuals who have founded it. It is their creation and they have to keep it alive in a civilization which is not congenial to family life.

In our Community we have larger families, we might call them "Camphill families," not created by blood bonds but by the spirit that unites us. While the natural family can be a gift to the wider Camphill family and Community, the Community in turn can embrace and support each natural family. This, in our experience, is a valid metamorphosis of old social forms, which were primarily blood ties, to new relationships which arise out of the allegiance of individuals to the spirit of the Community they have chosen to serve. Our attitudes to family life have a deep influence on those children and adolescents who are with us, as well as on our students and helpers. Some come from loving homes, others have experienced the break–up of their family and some have been rejected. It is part of our educational task of healing to include everyone, children and adults, into our house communities and imbue them with an experience of a spiritual family. To those who come from a background which seems to have failed them we take care not to express any judgment about their parents as this would only add insult to injury. Childhood deprivation is an injury as real as any physical injury, because every child longs to love his parents. Naturally we would build bridges whenever possible to re–establish a positive relationship, yet we cannot agree with the dogmatic approach of a certain present–day philosophy which states that every child *must* be with his parents. Some children are indeed better off away from their physical parents and some do not take well to adoptive parents. In our Community, children are accepted as persons in their own right and can feel part of us as a spiritual family. This can bring healing and leave them free to make their own way in life, when appropriate, knowing that we will accompany them as friends. The ultimate security we can offer to anyone is rooted in that Christian spirit which inspires us to trust in the meaningfulness of human destiny.

We are fortunate to be a colourful and yet coherent community of older and young people, including many staff families with children. These families are fully integrated into the wider family of the house community and, quite naturally, help our children and young people who are here as pupils to develop a feeling of trust and a sense of family. The "staff" children adopt the attitudes of their parents as a matter of course and, in our experience, accept the pupils on equal terms as people in the community. They are first and foremost children and adolescents on a voyage of growing up and of discovering the present day world and themselves. Difficulties arising between our staff children and pupils are no different from those which may occur among youngsters "down the road," or in any school playground. Our staff children have the advantage that they develop a natural understanding for their contemporaries who may have handicaps and they see in them people like themselves. Beautiful friendships can be experienced among children who grow up in such a community whether they have particular handicaps or not. The Community, in turn, has a responsibility towards the families in our midst. Their toddlers might not always be able to share meals with ten or twenty people in a large dining–room, and their older children — as indeed, our older pupils — may sometimes need an inner and outer space to be by themselves and develop their independence. Our staff children may see more of their parents than many others do but they have to share their attention with everyone else in the house. Thus we form extended families, created and fostered by those spiritual bonds of warm interest and active compassion, from which a staff family benefits as much as anyone else in the Community. When mother is ill or otherwise engaged, for example with the arrival of a new baby, there are always some co-workers, or one or the other older pupil, who will love to help with the children, so that father can continue teaching his class or working in the garden as he would normally do.

This spirit of mutuality is at the heart of, and makes possible, our considered policy of not segregating children according to the classification of learning difficulties or handicaps. It gives them a balanced experience of sharing life with people of different ages "at home" in their family houses and meeting their peers in the more formal setting of a classroom. It does make special demands on the flexibility and adaptability of our staff, but it has, over the past twenty five years (since 1964), proved to be of great value and help towards the maturation of our pupils. The relationships of the peer group and of younger and older pupils to one another is at least as important to a child's development as any influence brought to bear on him by his educators. It is, therefore, a special art to group children and young people in each house community and class so that they can best benefit from sharing life with one another. Awareness, tact and empathy towards the individual child and an almost intuitive appreciation of his personal destiny are required to do justice to him and the overall grouping of children and staff in our Schools' Community.

This process begins when we admit a pupil and try to place him into a group of children to whom he can give as much as he receives. Correspondingly, our admissions tend to reflect an effort to find those groupings in which just such mutual support will be best found. We have not, for example, found it helpful for any grouping in a house or a class to have more than a third of the children suffering from autism. In the right context even a child who has a severe contact disturbance can be of help to others and thereby have an experience of personal human value. If Mary, a child with Down's Syndrome, shares a room with autistically withdrawn Jeannie, Mary will not be put off by Jeannie's lack of response but will spare no effort to make and foster contact with Jeannie. In turn this increases Mary's own human potential and stature while it gives new meaning to Jeannie's life. However, when children with Down's Syndrome are among themselves in a group together they often deteriorate and lose their human dignity.

Similarly, it is not helpful if too many children with prickly mal-adjustment problems share a room, are in the same class or house since this merely enhances their maladjustment and encourages them to vie with and outdo each other in their unhelpful and destructive pursuits. Conversely, if there is only one child in a group who tries to compensate for his early childhood deprivation by appropriating other people's be-loved possessions he has a good chance of outgrowing this affliction. Everyone in the house will sense who the culprit is when something goes missing and this helps the child to improve his ways and use his capable hands to help others who are less able than he. He may develop a fine sense of compassion and personal dignity and in the end he might even be helpful to a new child who arrives with the very same problem which he has overcome. On the same basis, a child who is physically handi-capped can give much love and joy to another who has problems of maladjustment but is capable of assisting and caring for him. He knows that someone is worse off than he, so corrosive jealousies may be allevi-ated; both children thereby will experience increased meaningfulness in their lives which enhances their self-respect.

Special attention must be given to relationships which develop between adolescents and can cause severe problems unless we can guide them to keep their awakening sexuality and intellectual prowess in balance by developing a compassionate interest in the world, in every-thing that is human, whether far away or nearby. Such guidance is required even more when their intellectual ability is retarded or distorted. Destructive peer-group pressure on the one hand, and lonely self-concern on the other, can be dispelled by sharing discovery in learning and meeting others as well as in planning and carrying through of practical projects. Such sharing can be supported by drama or adventure groups which both offer good opportunities for group-discussions and mutual assessment. We take care that the senior pupils have their own life and activities within our house communities, but it is helpful for them to share the household with a group of younger children, so providing a natural incentive to practise self-restraint and take care of the younger ones. Once they realize that their example is important to younger children they are helped to improve their own conduct and to mature.

There is a fine dividing line between feeling responsible merely for one's own deeds and facing up to a responsibility for the life and well-being of others. Such a dividing line marks precisely the all–important transition from adolescence to adulthood, sometimes so hard to achieve. Our senior pupils, approaching this transition, often seek for real friendship and understanding among young adults who have just reached the other side of this subtle boundary. When all goes well the adolescent develops a certain dignity which far outweighs his handicap and the intellectual limitations he may have, whereupon he is truly ready to leave school.

To the young adult co–worker encounters of this kind can be an existential challenge which sets him upon a path of self–knowledge and self–education simply because this is what the adolescent seeks in his adult friend. And no adolescent will be impressed unless self–education is a matter of enthusiasm carried with a healthy sense of humour. Of course, this is not to say that children of all ages do not present a similar challenge to all who are adult. The young child tends to seek the shelter and security which can be offered by the more mature person who has gained that inner certainty which is able to create a protected space or, one could say, a "magic garden" wherein the child feels safe and free to play and to grow up. An older child and young adolescent often looks for the company and the example of the man or the woman in the middle of life, who are in their late twenties to early forties. Those children want and need to see how we adults handle things and cope with all the practical demands of human existence in the world of work, and it is just in the middle years of our life–span on Earth when our strength and skills are at their best.

Obviously we cannot be rigid about how different age groups affect each other but it is good to create situations in which children, young people and adults can find each other in significant relationships that further their human development. The recognition, among us adults, of our best potential corresponding to different ages allows us to support each other to the good and the wellbeing of everyone within the whole Community. We do not work for salary and promotion and thereby we are free to serve these needs according to our individual strengths and abilities, a pursuit which enhances the capacity of the individual and fosters warm mutual relationships. The older we grow the greater grows our privilege in that we can continue to learn and develop our humanity through our interaction with the Community. We do not have a retirement age and, when co–workers become frail and need assistance, we can care for them here. To meet old people and help care for them benefits those who are still young, and is part of healthy community life. The sharing of life and work in our extended families, and in the whole Schools' Community, is our joy and comfort, yet at the same time it is a daily challenge. It is a way of life, and while requiring continuous learning and achieving, sometimes results in failure, leading to new recognitions and renewed effort. We learn from each other, especially from the encounter with those children and adolescents who are entrusted into our care. They are the first to discover our frailties yet they are forgiving and, under all circumstances, expect us to set an example and guide them. It is more difficult for adults to extend this same magnanimous attitude towards each other. Undoubtedly our children lead the way in helping us to overcome our fears and faint–heartedness and to gain that courage which says: "Yes, I *can* devote myself to this task, truly and wholeheartedly."

The co–workers in a house community continually weave a supportive network of awareness, human warmth and active care around their group of children and for the environment formed by their house and garden. Areas or corners which slip our attention soon suffer from neglect and attract destructive and unhelpful behaviour. Our children and young people are even more vulnerable than others to this as their handicap makes them prone to slide all too quickly into harmful, if not dangerous, situations which would impair the development of their true human potential. In one instance a newly admitted boy with a history of epilepsy might have died if his housemother had not woken from sleep at 3 am, sensing that she must go to the boy, and found him in status epilepticus which needed medical intervention. Were it her own child a caring mother might have woken up to the emergency out of her motherly instinct, but we have to acquire such sensitivity, individually and as a group. If there had been a "hole" in that network of awareness the boy in his seizure might not have been discovered in time. Similarly, another child or youngster might abscond, or yet another, who gives no overt cause for concern, might not receive proper attention. This acquired sensitivity needs to be coupled with our knowledge and experience of diagnosing human handicaps and frailties. It makes us realize that we ourselves are all handicapped and frail in some way or other. Such recognition can become a stumbling block to an adult in the community if, as an individual, he feels too exposed and too harshly judged or judges himself too severely. It is similar to a marriage when, after the "honeymoon," the couple must learn to live with each other "for woe and for weal." As co-workers and members of the Camphill Community we share in spirit and practice the striving to accept the destiny of each individual who has joined us with his strengths, his endeavour and his frailties. We try to recognize the best in each other and to hold on to it faithfully once we have seen it. We know that all of us have times when we are weak and times when we are stronger, therefore, we depend on faithfulness towards each other.

Thomas Weihs, at a meeting of our Schools' Community during his last illness, spoke of our mutual encounter in life. He asked us to "enjoy the otherness of the other" and experience personal satisfaction in the progress which we see in others. Thereby we can give to the world, even if in a small measure, tolerance and love: those qualities for which there is so dire a need in our time.

# A community philosophy

Our social life and its administration are guided by three principles: brotherliness, freedom and equality, realizing that each of these pertains only to certain aspects of the social fabric of life. The economic life is based on the principle of *brotherliness*. Our individual requirements vary as do our abilities to contribute to the basic needs of our daily life and work but the economic life of the whole community is healthy to the extent that we can adhere to what Rudolf Steiner calls the Fundamental Social Law:

> In a community of human beings working together, the wellbeing
> of the community will be the greater, the less the individual
> claims for himself the proceeds of the work he has himself done;
> that is, the more of these proceeds he makes over to his fellow-
> workers, and the more his own requirements are satisfied, not out
> of his own work done, but out of the work done by the others.[10]

Obviously, this law cannot be used as a doctrine, neither can anyone be forced to live according to it. It can, however, be used as a practical guideline in a community which is such that each single member says: the communal body is as it should be and I *will* that it be thus. This is possible only when in every single member, down to the least, the spirit of the community is alive and active.

The spiritual and cultural life of our Community is guided by the principle of the *freedom* of the individual. The wellspring of our cultural life is found in the gifts and strengths of individuals, but their motivation and creativity can become effective only if it is reflected by the whole Community. In fact the response of the Community can pour cold water on ingenuity and innovative ideas or it can provide the fire that steels the will to forge our future. Spiritual life in our Community flourishes when we can grant freedom to each other, out of which we can unite in our will to do the good.

Between brotherliness and freedom stands *equality,* which should not be mistaken for sameness. Our needs and our gifts are different but, before God, human beings are equal. A certain equality, based on empathy and interest, is therefore applicable to all human relationships. It is to be hoped that this principle finds expression also in laws which are laid down by governments. However, the written and unwritten laws of human conduct and relationships are necessary and must be accepted as a reality for every small and larger community, but they change or metamorphose as human life and history evolve. Therefore we need to be sensitive to such changes and strive to ensure that concern and forgiveness override rigidity and habit in human interaction. This striving is the only guarantee that brotherliness and freedom can be kept in balance and that none of these three principles may dominate the other two. It must make certain that freedom does not deteriorate into a free-for-all, equality is not turned into sameness, and brotherliness cannot be distorted into "Big Brother" telling us what to do. Each of the three principles is applicable in its own sphere but these three spheres of social life interpenetrate in the daily life and work of the individual and of every group of people. Administration means literally to minister to, that is to serve, the community and it is helpful and healing if these three spheres can be seen clearly and handled separately. A growing task for the Camphill Community is to realize this way of administering and conducting its own affairs and, on a small scale, make it visible to the world. Camphill's setting enables those who live here, whether or not they have an overt handicap, to participate fully in its social fabric, to work according to their ability and thereby make a real contribution towards a social renewal in our time.

Membership of the Camphill Community is a commitment to uphold the image of Man and to serve the needs of our time. There is no contract or fee which would constitute membership but it is based on goodwill and on acceptance of responsibilities. All those who live and work here participate in the endeavour of our Community; everyone contributes something and receives something, but not everyone need commit himself to the Community. Those who are committed members meet and communicate in smaller or larger groups locally or worldwide. These groups foster our spiritual striving and our community awareness but they are not an aim in themselves because they exist to serve the needs of life and people in the world. Community members feel a responsibility to support and develop the institutions and social forms of the Community. They give their work without personal remuneration in the form of salaries, though their personal needs are met out of the income of the institutions the Community serves. This allows them to work freely and let their resources of ingenuity and goodwill flow into the work that needs to be done. They strive to increase their understanding of anthroposophy so that it becomes helpful in our work, in every aspect of our spiritual task and practical life. Knowledge and insight thus achieved are not then used for personal gain but can be applied in our educational and cultural endeavours, as well as in our practical work.

A special jewel in the life of the Camphill Community is the Bible Evening which is conducted in our house communities every Saturday. Every adult and occasionally senior pupils may participate. We gather and wait quietly before sitting at a table to have a simple meal and share in a conversation about any topic which moves our hearts then follow this by reading a chosen chapter of the Gospels. We share our thoughts and experiences about it. The Bible Evening is a moment of peace, allowing for an encounter from Ego to Ego, the unimpeachable spirit being within us, unencumbered by the hustle of daily life. It offers a holy space in which we can unite ever anew and from which strength and inspiration can flow into the week ahead. The Bible Evening, the services and the celebration of the festivals regularly reaffirm our human relationships and human values which are treasures in the life of every individual.

All who are part of modern society tend to suffer from "alienation": we can walk past each other though we meet daily at work, or even at home, and we can be alone amidst a crowd. True community can grow only when it is rooted in the individual who reaches beyond himself with human interest and who nurtures that inner flame which fills him with enthusiasm. Real interest can lead to an actual experience of the other person's situation, feelings and experiences. True enthusiasm goes beyond youthful fire and becomes an inner resource which will never burn out. These qualities are not given by nature: they are truly human and can only be achieved by faithful inner work and striving. Interest and enthusiasm are the wellspring of continually evolving community life: they create bonds which unite us whether we are young or old, nearby or far from each other; they allow human warmth and love to be the formative forces in personal and community life and striving. Members of the Camphill Community have to go through the same phases of development in their personal lives and have to face the same problems in themselves and in modern life as anyone else, but it is this endeavour of human interest and enthusiasm which allows a healing spirit to work with us, and this spirit is far greater than we are.

# 3 Education in the family group

## Care and guidance

The acknowledgment of the human spirit in the other person and the development of a true relationship to him are the basis of the care which we take on when admitting a child. A parent whose child has been with us for a few years described her experience of this in the following way:

> Since our child has attended your Schools our life has changed and we have discovered new human qualities. Previously, we were mainly concerned with our money, our house, our car and other material things. Now all this has become much less important and we have become increasingly grateful that we have this child. Even though it was a struggle, it was difficult and there may be more difficulties in the future, he has helped us to discover new values in life.

Such new values grow in us and our students as well as the parents when we seek to experience, in Karl König's words already quoted: "The encounter from Ego to Ego, from being to being." This is both philosophy and daily practice. Behind the veil of our shortcomings and, maybe, handicaps we are human beings who want to commune with one another. We can become particularly aware of this at certain times of the day when we are not formally teaching or educating but are caring for and about one another and that "veil" can be drawn away for a short moment. They are precious moments of mutuality between the child or young person and ourselves or his parents, moments of true encounter which kindle our awareness of one another's essential being, of that aspect in ourselves which goes through life, exists before we are born and will continue after we have died. To these rhythmically recurring moments belong the evenings when settling for sleep, the mornings when we encounter a new day, and meal–times.

Sleep can be called the little brother of death and waking–up the little sister of birth. The book of life is completed when a person dies and the script of destiny may reveal his true being. It is a special moment when we may see the wholeness of a life's panorama. It may convey to us something of the wholeness and true aims of a person's being. Every evening a page of the book of life is completed and we do well to be aware of it when we settle a child for the night. Every morning a new page is started, new images may become reality in the course of the day and we try to receive the child into it.

The following examples may illustrate some of the practical implica– tions. We endeavour to create for each child and young person, the possibility of closing his day and going to sleep in peace. Misdeeds can be forgiven, disappointments and anger, often about himself, can be left behind. Unsolved "knots" can be untied or cut, so that the child can relax. For our young children we create order and peace around them, making them feel embedded in human warmth. We light a candle, may tell them a story and thereby create a feeling of security, then play some gentle music and say prayers individually with each child. When they are adolescents, it can be all important to have individual quiet conversa– tions, guided by our awareness of each young person's needs. The one may need to look back on the day past and be reassured: "Well, this is how it was and we can now not change it. It is over; leave it, let it go and make peace with yourself and the world." Another may be not so concerned about the past but more than apprehensive about the next day: he is over–sensitive and cannot go to sleep, worrying about what might happen tomorrow. Therefore his group–parent has to reassure him, telling him that she will wake him in the morning, accompany him when he rises, that they will have breakfast together and then he will go to the classroom. Every evening he needs to be guided to look at the usual events which will happen the next day, even though they occur every day. Of course, this needs to be followed up the next day. If unforeseen circumstances cause a change of the expected events he needs special help otherwise he feels extremely insecure and might react with social or even physical aggression. Such small details are of great importance to all children, even more so for children who have special needs. We have to adhere to them for years, for many years. They help to develop a protective "skin" around the inner sensitivity of the growing child and adolescent so that eventually he can establish himself in this life. Such a skin can be likened to the boundary of touch, where he becomes aware of the world around.

With equal care we try to receive children into the day. It is helpful to awaken them gently. Therefore a recorder or flute is played through the house before opening the curtains or switching on the light. We may find a young restless child who has jumped out of his bed because he woke early; him we have to ease into the day so that he can come to breakfast without squealing or throwing his plate across the dining–room. There may be a young person who, due to his deprived background, has difficulty facing the day: he does not want to get up because he does not want to be the boy with an ugly face, as he experiences himself, he just does not want to be this person again today. Therefore, we have to extend our warmth and reassure him so that he can face the day without feeling impelled to reinforce his poor self–image by doing something ghastly. All too often he has experienced people saying that he is a horror and this tends to become a self–fulfilling prophesy. In a subtle, quiet way we make sure that he feels warmly accepted and supported to become the better self he would like to be.

Breakfast and all meal–times belong to the rhythmically recurring events of the day which, however, are social occasions, shared by the entire house community. The beauty and care with which a meal is prepared, surrounded and conducted, and meal–time conversations have a deep influence on everyone's wellbeing. All these are taken in and "digested" with the food and create deeply rooted social habits in our lives. Conducting a meal is an art in itself. First the whole house community gathers and when the last stragglers have arrived some medicines may be given out. We then proceed into the dining–room, everyone to his place where he finds his napkin bag with his name embroidered on it. An all important moment of silence precedes grace after which the dishes are collected from the oven and a table conversation can ensue in which joys and sorrows of the day can be shared. If tables are round, some six to eight children and adults can listen to each other and share in one conversation. At the end of a meal we repeat what we did at the beginning: we all take hands, wait until everyone is quiet and then give thanks for the meal. On Sundays or festive occasions the blessing may be sung. The habit of observing a moment of quiet before and after a meal strengthens our ability to listen. Listening is the soil out of which meaningful conversation can grow naturally. This shows, for example when visitors remark that our children can sit through long performances of plays and music much better than children who have no such handicaps. Meal–times also offer a precious opportunity to develop dexterity and social graces by observing good table manners. John who is thirteen has needed a long time to teach his fingers how to hold a knife and fork correctly. Now he uses his great energy in upholding what he has learned but cutting his meat and vegetables, without pushing them off the plate, still needs that extra effort. His outbursts of temper have almost ceased; reminders and praises from the teacher who sits next to him are accepted in good humour. He has also learned to pronounce her name correctly but he continues, with a broad smile, to say ".orma" instead of "Norma" or ask for a "nabana" (banana).

Irvine, a fourteen–year–old, who recently came to us, is conscious of being overweight and is modest in his food intake. He uses the opportunity of a table conversation to make contact with an older staff member sitting next to him: "Did you know I had an accident during holidays when I was five years old, I ran into a car?" It was his way of asking: "Did you know I sustained a brain injury?" Then, a reassuring conversation about his home and the large extended family ensued. After this he was asked if he minded sharing a room with David, a boy suffering from a progressive illness and needing complete physical care. Irvine's definite reply was: "It is a privilege," thereby expressing recognition that it was helpful to him. He had been expelled from his previous school as an exhibitionist but here, through sharing with David and helping to care for him, this problem was dispelled.

Catherine is now a young lady, full of outgoing human contact and fun even though she has little word understanding and cannot speak. She "converses" in shrieks of joy or disgust making clear to everyone what she feels like today. A few years ago, when she first came, she behaved as if she were a wild animal showing little interest in human beings, screaming, smearing her faeces and tearing her clothes. Now she is a cheerful person and no longer disrupts meal–times. Charles, sitting at another table, together with the three young children of the houseparents, used to be a trial to everyone because of his hyperactivity; there is a suggestion that he was a battered child. One day he refused to come into the dining–room and tried to defy any adult interference. Later in the day, a teacher who does not otherwise look after him but sits next to him at the table, took him aside and quietly said to him: "I really miss you when you don't come to a meal." The following day at lunch time,

Charles asked this teacher: "And what have you been doing this morning?" Charles did not miss a meal again, at least, not for a long time. A house community of children and adults can develop a great tolerance and also skill in coping with the restlessness of young children, emotional outbursts of adolescents or even epileptic seizures, all of which may occur at table. Then there is a spirit of natural acceptance and support, acting as is appropriate to the situation and then continuing the meal in peace. On Sundays and at festivals, meal–times are central social occasions where human warmth and home culture can unite everyone.

True integration, as we see it, begins with mutual encounter and develops into a maturation process as we try to meet the needs of others. The interaction between children who have different needs and problems can be particularly helpful here. A few examples may illustrate our ways of guiding and encouraging this process. Mary, a girl of fifteen with Down's Syndrome used to be at home, loved and well cared for, but doing nothing herself. She was overweight and had a weak heart. After a year with us she was moved into a room with a little seven–year–old girl who suffered from a severe psychotic condition, screaming at night, tearing everyone's belongings and throwing her excrement through the room unless she was watched all the time. From the first day on, Mary loved this little girl and in the course of the second year, she became a faithful nanny to Jeannie so that a beautiful relationship developed to the benefit of both. Mary learned to do things just because they needed to be done and Jeannie responded to the loving attention given to her day and night by the older girl which helped her to calm down considerably. Of course, it needed careful guidance by the group parent and the house-parents, especially to see that Mary was not overstrained. Without Jeannie, Mary could never have achieved the human maturity that became a radiant strength of hers.

Eric came to us as a frail thirteen–year–old with a slight stammer and a habit of retiring to bed with a tummy–ache when life was too much for him. Soon he expressed his appreciation of our broad school syllabus: he so much enjoyed geography, history and sciences that he forgot about his tummy–aches. One evening in a gathering of the adolescent boys in the house, they were asked by the housefather to describe how they experienced each other. Some of them had severe behavioural problems, especially Peter whose father had died and whose mother, a hard woman, rejected him. All of them spoke with a certain respect of Eric while making some guarded, but less respectful remarks about one another.

Then finally, Eric was encouraged to speak for himself. He described in simple words and with great clarity, the positive potentials of each of the other boys, contrasting these against their repeated attempts to maltreat him. From that time onwards, Eric became the moral backbone of the group and Peter developed a feeling of deep gratitude towards him. A year after leaving school Peter was caught stealing and had to spend time in prison but there is hope that he will eventually stabilize and make use of the values absorbed here. Eric's perception of human needs had grown to an inner strength that gained him respect amongst his workmates.

Violence and self–destruction can cause severe problems here as everywhere else in our time. Having to discharge an adolescent because he has become a threat to other pupils can cause great stress to the young person himself as well as our staff and the wider community in the country. It does not occur often but when it does, we (and the sending authority) are faced with our limits. At present, individuals who are a danger to themselves and society can be sent to "secure" accommodation only through a court order which, tragically, means: only after they have committed a crime. However, we will not give up trying to improve our understanding and methods to meet individual situations. A most potent healing factor for overcoming, or better still, preventing aggression is building up adequate human relationships. The following three examples can illustrate different aspects of our work in this respect.

Joseph was referred to us at the age of nine, a dark–haired, red–faced, exceptionally strong and active young lad. A psychiatrist asked him to explain a picture he had drawn and his reply was: "It's an elephant's ear hiding behind a tree." Joseph's imagination could outshine the dark and stark reality of his family background. By the time he was twelve there was no–one in the family who would have him for a holiday or take a real interest in him. In that year he grew and matured physically into the appearance of a strong sixteen–year–old but intellectually he was at an average level of a ten–year–old and emotionally he had not yet outgrown the reactions of a young five–year–old — a desperate situation to live with. At the age of thirteen he had reached such a state of inner conflict that there was not a day without tempers. He needed a period of strict holding and restraining, after which he made good progress in adjustment and gradually brought the different levels of his maturing personality into better harmony. Naturally his social worker and ourselves were concerned to prepare the way for his school leaving as there was no way of holding Joseph back. Not only was he determined to leave at sixteen but he even rejected the financial support and the relatively good bedsit which the social work department had arranged for him. He felt he had no family and so he was going to make his own way. Three years later he visited to introduce his fiancée, a girl from a caring and settled home background; they then set up home together.

Problems of violence can arise due to an autistic or psychotic type of disturbance. Stewart, coming from a caring and protective home, was admitted at the age of ten. On arrival here, while his houseparents were talking with his father, he roamed the school grounds, smashed a dozen clay couplings for drain pipes and threw a workman's jacket into a fire. Once he had settled at Camphill, his housemother regularly told him special stories about a boy who learnt to keep his hands out of mischief and taught them instead to do good work for other people. Some months later she found him walking up and down a passage looking intently at his hands. When questioned what he was doing his reply was: "Don't distract me, I must guard my hands." On another occasion he had destroyed a number of newly planted trees. A few days later, in the middle of the day, he seemed to have disappeared and was eventually found in his bed with his blankets over his head. Asked why he had gone to bed he explained: "I must keep myself out of mischief." In time destructiveness ceased entirely and as he grew into adolescence he became almost over–controlled. He was good at manual skills to the extent that he could use a saw as if he were a trained joiner but he had great difficulty in learning to understand the motivation required to integrate his activity into an everyday work situation. The I–You relationship remained a problem for him. He could, by way of his intellectual understanding, use the personal pronouns correctly but in his emotional experience they remained unclear and this made life difficult for him. One morning he came into his housefather's room saying: "Good morning, Henry. How am I?" When the housefather looked at him questioningly, he eventually explained that he meant to say: "How are you?" As a young adult Joseph learned to drive a car with skill and confidence through the centre of London but he could not pass a driving test because he did not understand why he should answer the driving instructor's questions when the instructor already knew the answers!

We should not meet aggression with aggression, but this is easier said than done. Curt had stolen Leslie's watch and Jimmy found it in Curt's locker. A little later a fight developed between Curt and Leslie (both being seventeen years old) and Jimmy enjoyed watching this, from a safe distance. The housemother, being pregnant at that time, entered the boys' room and calmly told Leslie: "Go into my room, I will talk with you later," and sent Curt outside to chop wood. The boys did not argue but simply did as they were told. Such actions are based on human confidence which has been built up over a period of time. Any shadow of fear on the part of the housemother would have undermined this. If a less experienced but physically strong young man had entered that room he might well have got involved in the fight, being unable to separate the two boys. Situations of this kind are a great challenge to the emotional strength and balance of our co-workers.

A last example about a boy with severely self-destructive tendencies. He had a sleep problem, was "seeing" ghosts coming out of the wall and would desperately bang his forehead against hard surfaces. His saving graces were inventiveness and humour. Sebastian was nine years old and had not been here for long. He chose to call his housemother by her surname although we all address each other by our Christian names. Sebastian appeared in his housemother's bedroom at 3 am, saying: "Mrs Martin, can I put your big toe into the fridge?" The following night, round the same time Sebastian appeared again, saying: "Mrs Martin, can I put your head into the fridge?" He was prevailed upon not to wake people during the night unless he was unwell or needed help. The third night he was found on the swing outside the house. Very astonished he said to his housemother: "How did you notice? I went out very quietly and just wanted to swing in the moonlight."

# Social training and work

Emma, eight years of age, had the task of putting out the bedroom slippers for herself and the three companions with whom she shared a room. It took her a few months to learn which slippers belonged to whom, where they should be put, also when to collect and put them away again in the morning. After two terms she was able to change to a new task and learn to empty the contents of the wastepaper basket and the bin from the bathroom into the big bin outside, without spilling the contents onto the ground, even without getting lost on the way. Stephen who was twelve, remarked: "I have swept these stairs every morning for a whole year," and the housefather replied: "Yes, and we all have enjoyed going up and down a clean staircase." This remark of Stephen's was an important moment in his moral development, the recognition of his ability to do something for others regularly and reliably. It is part of our practice that household chores, cooking, working on the land and in the maintenance workshops are shared with our children and young people. We wish to give them the experience that work is something we do for others and that each one of us depends on the work done by others for us. Many of our young people who are prospective school leavers, spend a year going out for work experience with local employers. Sharon, a girl with Down's Syndrome, had a term's work experience at a local supermarket. She was liked and appreciated by the staff there and at the end of that period was brought home by them with a car load full of presents for her companions here and a letter of re-commendation, for reliable work and friendliness, from the manager. However, Graham's first work experience was at a garage, where, after a couple of weeks, the manager asked that the boy be withdrawn because he would not listen to what he was told and wanted to use abrasive material for cleaning a customer's car. In the weekly evening meetings of senior pupils, Sharon and Graham had important experiences to share with each other: this helped Graham considerably and his second place-ment was more successful.

The steps on the way from Emma looking after the bedroom slippers to Sharon and Graham working with local tradesmen may take some ten years. The success depends primarily on developing a good working morale and sociability. We endeavour to instil into our children and young people an experience of caring for one another as well as for the place we live in.

Young children naturally imitate the adults' way of working and car-ing. As they grow up they can develop a sense of self-respect based on the discovery of their own potential to do things for others. Children naturally want to work for their teacher in class and their houseparents in the house, who in turn do well to accept this tactfully and express their appreciation. Thereby children can develop a healthy self-respect which in their adolescence can become the basis for their working morale. The attitude that work is doing something for others will then be natural to these young people's character and often they are appreciated for it.

Employers may find it worthwhile to make special allowances for their handicap and slightly odd behaviour. This happened to a former pupil who is a foreman at a sawmill, even though he cannot read or write, but he supports his mates with his enthusiasm for their work.

The development of *motivation,* as described above, is part of our general curriculum and the development of manual skills is systematically used as part of our extended classroom syllabus. Young children start with handwork lessons, from twelve upwards woodwork is added and the older ones are taught basic crafts, such as simple joinery, metalwork, weaving, basketry and candle–making. The articles produced are pleasing and can be used as presents. Cooking and baking are taught "at home" in the houses rather than in the classroom and some senior pupils may spend a period as kitchen helpers. Gardening and working with animals start for young children as a regular weekly activity while some adolescents are greatly helped by working alongside a gardener or farmer in the afternoons. In the Upper School our pupils have block periods in all these crafts and in domestic and outside work but in their final year our senior pupils can specialize according to their aptitudes. There are good possibilities for training in the Schools' own building and maintenance workshop as well as in our gardens, smallholding and households. Those who gain sufficient independence to work in the open community may spend a whole year having work experience with different local employers. A letter of recommendation from one or two of these employers can be worth more for the young person's prospects of employment than a school leaving certificate.

A young person who may be able to work but who cannot adequately integrate socially is not yet employable. Most of our school leavers can work but many need more time before they can hold their own in the open society or settle down in a village community. Their way to independence is long and arduous and, therefore, we see the training of social integration as being of equal importance as learning to work. Naturally, this way starts within the house community and the class. It is regularly tested when children go home for holidays, in their meeting with the family and its local environment; but here within the Schools too we can gradually widen the social circumference of the child. Emma may be sent with a note to the neighbouring house and asked to bring back a reply; Stephen may be sent to the garden to fetch some vegetables from the gardener; Charles may be asked one day of the week to go, on his own, to feed the horses; Irvine can be sent, on his bicycle, for messages to local shops or to the Schools' other estate three miles away. Some of our adolescents learn to go on their own to the local library and eventually they can take the bus and go to town to do their own shopping on Saturdays. With our help, pupils run their own clubs for swimming, basketball and other sports and social activities. For some of them, it is essential that they go out independently and join local young people who do not have handicaps. We support them individually to become members of a Scout Troop, youth group or a similar organization. All these are small but important stepping stones towards independence.

# Play and social maturation

Play is a serious necessity for the child. If he cannot play his development will be impaired, if not stunted altogether. Many children at our Schools cannot play adequately due to their handicap or lack of stimulation in early childhood. Their spontaneous ability to play creatively may have been even further impaired by uncontrolled viewing of television rather than being involved in social interaction and play with the family and neighbours. The result can be a growing apathy or hyperactivity; some children swing between these two extremes. Therefore, we have to *teach* many of our children how to play and be creative. This is not merely a free time activity but pertains to the whole day even though, as it were, it goes underground when the child participates in a formal lesson or while he is asleep. A child's sleep is healthier when he has played and in a lesson he can make better use of what is imparted to him. He can absorb it with an active imagination and take hold of the world through his ability to imitate.

Some examples may illustrate ways of helping children to play. Lee, nine years of age, suffers from autism and neurological injury. His ability to imitate is severely reduced and consequently his movements, his speech and his thought life are hindered in their development. In order to help him, and other such children, we played movement games, freely invented or traditional, such as "Pat–a–cake, pat–a–cake, baker's man" followed by ring games ("Ring–a–ring–a–roses"). He was delighted once he had discovered the possibility of "falling down dead and rising again." The further steps were ring games in which a child acts in the centre ("Old Roger is dead") and then the ring was opened ("In and out the windows" or "Mousey, mousey come out of your housey"). It took a long time for Lee to dare sit in the middle of the ring and it took him even longer to accept the idea that the ring could be opened and that he could wind in and out, run away or catch somebody. A further step was forming two groups ("Here we come gathering nuts in May") and this led on to giving individuals such tasks as would sharpen their senses, for example "Blind Man's Buff." Lee learned to participate as part of a team but could not bear being blindfolded. His older friend Angus, who had similar difficulties but had better developed speech, was so sensitive that he could, even when he was securely blindfolded, call out correctly the name of anyone coming near to him. The way leads from mastering one's limbs and body movements, to sharing the security of a ring, to standing as an individual in the centre of the still secure ring and eventually to opening up the shelter of the circle and exploring the world with the help of our senses and our growing skill. This process can have innumerable variations and we need not be set on traditional patterns only; but there is great wisdom in the wealth of old nursery rhymes and games which can feed the imagination of both children and their teachers.

Healthy young children play the whole day long. Whatever they do is accompanied by their own creative imagination which is not always accessible to adults. Children who have to struggle with impairments may need help to develop such imaginations. Rising from bed in the morning was difficult for Billy. He was confused and seemed to be scattered all over the place. His group parent conducted Billy's morning as a game of going on a journey, making new discoveries when he was going to wash and brush his teeth. Beverley used to build up emotional barriers and became destructive at bedtime but was greatly helped by imagining a return to the harbour after a long journey or landing at the airport and having a reunion with trusted people. Damian, who is twelve, a little older than the other two, thought going for a walk through the Schools' grounds was a boring affair but he became enthusiastic about it when he learned to see the wonders of nature and find new things, stones, conkers, leaves, branches with special shapes and when coming back, using these to build imaginative houses, cities, vehicles, and so on.

A more severe problem arises when a child who did not play creatively approaches adolescence. Annika was nearly thirteen but retained features of a young infant's expanded consciousness. She loved helping with younger children, playing the many ring games which speak of death and weeping ("Poor Jenny sits a–weeping") and the search for the "true love." It helped her to develop a centred awareness of self and bear, even at her age, the pain of losing a young child's direct experience of the width and the light of the spirit from whence we came. Her soul was the "princess," the girl who wept or was dying but will find again her "true love," the "prince" who is her true spiritual self. Such games are usually played with children before they reach the second dentition but when they are older and have never played, they can, in our experience, still benefit from them up to the age of nine or ten. Once they are as old as Annika they can still be helped when they are given a chance to "help" playing such games with younger children.

For children who are fully in adolescence it is difficult, if not impossible, to make up for what they have missed as natural and healthy play in early childhood: they might need specialized play and drama therapy. In adolescence certain aspects of play transform into the young person's ability to apply himself to work. His powers of concentration and forethought, imagining the results of what he is doing, belong to this. Some young people who suffer from childhood autism find a new fulfilment when they can work. Some may become excellent gardeners or keep the shelves in a food store in perfect order but this is a one-sided development which, by itself, does not foster their social integration. In our experience in Village Communities with adults who have mental handicaps, these young adults are in danger of growing into social isolation or even suffering a mental breakdown in their late twenties, the age when our natural resources show the first signs of decline and we can no longer count on youthful impulses and original gifts. They then find themselves lonely while their contemporaries can rely on what they have built up in their twenties, such as a family, close social relationships, acquired abilities at work and enjoyable free time pursuits and hobbies. Some adolescents therefore, need continued help to transform those aspects of play which lead them into social life. Social games and certain table games may still widen their knowledge and experience of adapting to life in general. Hobbies and primarily non-competitive sports are also of value here. In our Schools we can offer swimming, basketball, rounders, riding, folk-dancing, music-making, hiking, camping and other activities. In the neighbourhood, Scouts, Guides, sports and youth clubs, children's and young people's orchestras can be joined on an individual basis. In addition to all these our house communities may take up seasonal activities such as hiking, camping, rehearsing songs or plays and making decorations for festivals. All these foster the social maturation of the individual.

# Toys, pets and books

Susan, ten years old, had a computerized "perfect" doll which was lying in a "perfect" cot in the girls' room. She played with it for a few days when it was new, then it was forgotten and none of her playmates looked at it either. A few weeks later she discovered a simple rag doll and took it into her bed. It was then given to her and she treasured it, having long conversations with this doll, dressing her in imaginative clothes, sharing joys and sorrows with her and finding much comfort in this companion. The "perfect" doll hindered Susan's creativity because it did not give her a chance to develop her imagination. A good toy stimulates imagination and inventiveness.

Sebastian came at the age of eight, bringing a whole collection of plastic and tin toys, carefully counted and listed by his parents who felt "at their wits' end" with him because of his hyperactivity, fixations and head banging. Within two months his toys were all destroyed or lost. We then gave him a large wooden train set and a bag full of felt and leather scraps with which to make things. These were not broken but gave him the first incentive for constructive activity, the beginning of his long way towards independence. Playing imaginatively and making things out of his felt scraps allowed Sebastian to free himself from his anxieties and fixations, to begin with for short periods. As he grew up these "spaces" of freedom grew wider and allowed him to turn creatively to the "real" world as he had turned to his toys. When he was in his mid–twenties he was able, against the odds of his impairment and with the support of his mother and sister, to establish himself in his own flat and shape his own life independently. The skills and powers of imagination which unfold when playing with toys in early childhood later transformed to become the hidden resources of the adolescent which support him in developing an interest in the world and empathy for others. In early adulthood these inner resources transform again and become a creative strength in shaping one's own life and personality within the wider society.

Christian, who was seventeen, a boy with superior intelligence but needing our care while working for his Scottish Higher examinations at a local comprehensive school, still held on to a fair–sized, tattered, old teddy which had to be near his bed. It was for him invested with loving warmth and gentleness which he had missed in his childhood, its texture and warm material were still important to him. Only when he left at the age of eighteen and felt ready for the next step in life could he forget the teddy and leave it behind in the corner of his wardrobe.

Similarly, pets can give comfort and can teach us to care. George, twelve years old, had missed the magic of childhood and had grown up in the world of stark realities. He pretended to be hard and tough, could kick a ball but could not use his hands to throw or catch it, let alone to caress a pet. He recklessly tore round on a bicycle but was unable to care for it or repair it. It was a surprise to him when he learned to swim, to play volley ball and was taught creative hobbies in the evenings. He continued expressing his anger and defiance by kicking and lashing out at others, but simultaneously his otherwise well hidden longing for gentleness was lavished on a jealously guarded pet rabbit. In time he learned to care for horses, became an ardent swimmer and forgot all about kicking and football. In another effort of self–healing he began to help caring for our grounds. Some years later, now employed as a street sweeper he visited his teacher who had been ill and came in his own car, accompanied by his slightly "handicapped" dog.

Another essential feature of our home life is story telling and reading. Janet, ten years old, took in her evening story as food and drink for her inner self. She still wanted to hear the same story over and over again as would be appropriate for a younger child. She and other children loved to go along with the seasons, listening in winter to stories such as Selma Lagerlöf's *The Christmas Rose* or in autumn to the legends of St George fighting the dragon and freeing the princess. Important milestones of progress and self–esteem were reached when Damian, Billy and Beverley in turn wanted to look at books and eventually could read stories for themselves. It was a great moment when Damian was trusted to go on his own to the town library and take out books of his choice. The ability to choose a good book and enjoy independent reading is an important aim of our education.

Also for older pupils, including those who can read for themselves, the ancient art of story telling can be helpful. In autumn, as the days became shorter and it was not opportune to play outside, George and other ado-lescents had regular evening sessions in which the whole of Homer's *Iliad* was told to them. They became so deeply absorbed in the story that they forgot their ingrained emotions of opposition and unruly behaviour. For a long time George thought the storyteller was telling her own stories and he was deeply astonished and moved when he realized that these were ancient stories which had accompanied and educated humankind throughout the course of millennia. He could express his appreciation and feel a little more "at home" in sharing life with humankind on Earth.

# Pastoral care

A curative educator practises pastoral care throughout the day when she spends her time with children but also when she is alone because it becomes part of an inner attitude. Before going to sleep in the evening she tries to picture in her mind the children and young people who are in her care, tries to see them as they are at present and also to imagine what the child's own ideal picture of himself and his aims in life might be. The curative educator takes care not to mix her personal desires and wishes into this exercise but she tries to surround the child with her concern and human warmth. We are usually called upon to intervene and change the course of a child's or young person's life and we try to direct this change towards what we can glean as a child's own ideal of himself. After such an exercise is regularly practised in the evening, the curative educator is in a better position on the following day to guide the children. She may meet the child at the right moment, be in the right place and just find a helpful word to say; she may discover a new method or a new therapy which is needed for a child at a particular time: often it can be a subtle word or remark, at other times it can involve vital occurrences, such as may be illustrated by the following two examples.

Barry was just five, unable to speak and extremely hyperactive. He had attended nursery class in the morning and now it was lunch time. Between having his face and hands washed and going down the stairs to the dining-room he disappeared. Within a few moments a search was arranged but no-one could find him in the house or in the Schools' grounds. His teacher went out again to search once more, the same area in the grounds which had been combed through before. When listening carefully he heard a tiny sound and then discovered Barry sitting in a shallow brook, hidden under an overhanging clump of earth below the roots of a tree, cold and ready to be found.

Often, essential pastoral conversations take place, by the way, while we are washing up, cleaning the house, working in the gardens, sitting at breaktime together at the kitchen table or in the garden shed. What matters is that the curative educator learns not to judge the person and not to react emotionally, but to be observant and alert at all times, trying to place herself into the situation of the child or young person and then, out of understanding thus gained, helping him to change, mature and realize his own aims in life. This is not a question of applying a simple reward and punishment scheme but it reaches far deeper layers of our existence. The reward lies in the progress and realization of true achievements and in building up warm mutual human relationships which involve more than one person alone.

It was hard to like Ian because his behaviour was so utterly despicable. At the age of fifteen he cruelly maltreated children who were weaker than he to the extent that he would push pins into them unless he was constantly observed. He stole like a magpie and it was not pleasant to sit next to him because he suffered from chronic constipation and repeatedly soiled himself. He was pale, thin and awkward in his movements. When an adult spoke to him he went into an emotional spasm, turning away, closing his mouth tightly and pressing his lips together so that they went blue. Any present he was given he would break almost instantly. Stephen, a boy of the same age was skilful and meticulous in anything to which he put his mind but social warmth was not his strength. He gladly agreed, however, to help Ian build a bicycle for himself out of bits and pieces from old bikes. No one among the staff could have afforded the same care, diligence and time to guide and work with Ian: each small piece had to be cleaned, repainted, oiled. Stephen knew every screw and bolt in his workshop corner and therefore it was impossible for Ian to steal anything because Stephen would notice immediately and demand it back. The bicycle, constructed through several months of work was then relatively well cared for by Ian.

However, communication with Ian remained very difficult but his housefather could open up a channel of conversation because Ian constantly desired this or that and therefore, would come and ask for a piece of string, scissors, glue or paper. These were opportunities used to ask him about his own life and experiences. He had been cruelly maltreated by his father and it was too late to replace what he had missed in early childhood. However, there was one person whom he loved dearly and who also was fond of him: that was his brother Alexander. Where Ian was dark, Alexander was fair and able to be a little more pleasant to people. He was boarding at another school and used to come to spend part of his holidays with us, the other part they spent together with their mother. In a conversation, Ian's housefather asked Alexander about his future plans and then asked him: "What do you think will happen to Ian if he continues stealing and maltreating people?" After a short pause the answer was: "I think he will go to prison." Alexander, then just thirteen, realized that he might be the person who could help his brother. The housefather responded: "The next time when Ian has stolen something ask him to give it back." He knew that the brothers had no secrets between each other. This was successful. When Alexander came to visit again he was told that Ian had stopped stealing and was casually asked by the housefather: "And what about you Alexander? Have you also stopped stealing?" He looked up in great astonishment and after thinking for a moment he realized that also he himself had begun to overcome this affliction. Both boys had lapses but eventually succeeded in freeing themselves from their deep–seated kleptomaniac tendencies. The ancient question: "Am I my brother's keeper?" stirred in the hearts of the fair and the dark brother and allowed a third one, the invisible companion of Man to bring healing to both and yet leave each one free. It belongs to pastoral care not to judge who of us is the fair or the dark one, who of us knows better or is right or wrong: the task is to open the door to the "inner room" for the healer to enter. Pastoral care as described here is part of the community life in which we all share.

# Religious education and experiences

Weekly non–denominational Christian lay services and celebration of Christian festivals marking the seasons of the year are intrinsic to life in our Community. Plays, pageants, music, with teachers and pupils uniting in their preparation and performance, are part of this. They engender human values and the memory of such shared experiences is a wellspring of inner security throughout life. Traditional plays are performed and new ones created, songs and choirs rehearsed, pictures painted and special decorations made to adorn the houses and classrooms for each festival.

Sunday services, conducted by members of our Community, are celebrated in three groupings: for younger children, for adolescents from fourteen upwards, and for senior pupils from sixteen years of age together with staff who wish to participate. We give religion lessons in

small and intimate groupings according to age in which significant conversations with and among our children and adolescents can arise. For
those who cannot easily participate because they are too restless or have
little word understanding we have a special puppet theatre for younger
ones and eurythmy performances for adolescents, in which religious
contents can be beautifully and artistically presented.

Another aspect of this, fostered in our home life, is individual conversation about prayer and personal questions arising, perhaps, through birth
and death experienced in the family or in the community. Religion, however, is an ingredient of our whole life not only of separate occasions. A
religious attitude which upholds the ideal image of Man and nurtures
human values, can permeate every lesson in class, be it sciences, humanities or art, and equally our activities in home life and leisure time. This
attitude is enhanced by the celebration of festivals. The seasons and their
festivals have a rhythmical "curriculum" of their own which is probably
as old and as transformed as humankind on Earth. It is valid for young
and old people alike but it needs to find new expressions as human
history evolves.

In the present age an awareness of the Earth as a living being is rising
in the modern mind like a "groundswell." We realize that our human
organism is part of this Earth and each individual has a responsibility to
care for the Earth as well as one's own body. It seems that in olden times
we had a more instinctive and atavistic experience of the living Earth
and it was then natural to express our allegiance and gratitude to God the
Creator and his great servants who maintain and renew our lives and the
Earth itself. In our time children may still have a natural perceptiveness
for such experiences but as we grow up much inner work and effort is
required to develop an understanding for the connection between our
spiritual origin and the aims of our life on Earth. The festivals, taken
seriously, have become a challenge to our warmth of heart and our
clarity of mind. Many old traditions seem to have lost their meaning and
what were "holy spaces" in the natural rhythm of the year have become
"hollow spaces" filled with commercialism. Therefore we endeavour to
create anew the seasonal festivals to be wellsprings in our lives and to
build bridges of human activity spanning across death and rebirth in Man
and nature. They can continually renew the meaning of our lives and
help us to overcome the deeply rooted fear of the modern person that
when the Earth eventually dies we may have lost our connection with the
spirit whence we came and to which we long to return. We shall now

attempt a brief survey of the festivals in our communal life and educational endeavour.

Christmas is a festival of finding a home on Earth. And those who come to Camphill, young or old, usually have first to experience Christmas in the Community before they can feel at home in Camphill. The celebrations begin on the first Advent Sunday with the Advent Garden: a large spiral of moss laid out on the floor, adorned with crystals, with a large candle burning on a tree stump in the centre, the only light in the room. Each child in turn is given a red apple with a white candle in it to carry along the inward spiralling path to the centre. There he lights it and on his way out, places it somewhere into the spiral of moss. Everybody else sits around the spiral of greenery singing Christmas carols to accompany the children on their special path. Some may have difficulty in their movements or spatial orientation and may need help, others who feel confident, are in such a rush that their candle goes out before they have set it down, but most of them achieve a dignity and concentration which touches the heart of the onlooker. In the end the whole room is filled with the gentle light of many candles and we can feel prepared to walk the path of Advent from the darkness of the world to the inner light of Christmas.

Everyone is involved in making decorations , such as transparencies and drawings of Christmas images, in practising songs, rehearsing plays, and each house has its own home–made Advent calendar so that each day one child, usually starting with the youngest, can open a window. On Christmas Eve the whole Community assembles in our Hall to participate in a Christmas pageant, beginning in darkness and ending with the glorious light of many candles on the large Christmas tree radiating through the Hall. From each family house one child has brought a lantern in which to carry the flame back to the smaller Christmas tree in the house for more intimate celebrations. The pageant was first written by Karl König and has since been re–written and re–composed almost year by year, so the spirit of it is fully alive, traditional as well as new each year.

Most children and older pupils stay to participate in our celebrations and then go home to be with their families. The adults continue to meet under the Christmas tree, studying and practising arts and music together throughout the time of the thirteen Holy Nights which ends with Epiphany, 6th January. We see Advent as a time of inner preparation which calls for inner search and struggle. Can we renew our allegiance to the Earth and our love for it as a home for the child, the promise of the future? The stable, a place of poverty in which the Christ Child is born, can be seen as an image of an historical event yet can be experienced also as a place within every human being today and in the future. The poorness of the heart begging for the light and the healing warmth of the spirit are very personal and at the same time generally human experiences. The green tree erected inside the house and the warm intimate light of its candles signify the renewal of life and strength in Man and in the Earth. For children this can be a natural experience but when we have grown up we have to work and strive for it each and every year anew.

At midsummer when we live in the season opposite to Christmas and the longest day in the northern hemisphere has just passed, we mark the St John's festival on 24th June, traditionally the birthday of John the Baptist. Outside, under the summer sky and again involving everyone, we perform a pageant and conclude it with a picnic, singing and folk-dancing which might carry on until deep into the night. At the height of summer, in the midst of the holiday mood which then begins to prevail, the voice of St John crying in the "wilderness": "change your ways" can be heard by all of us. Is the "wilderness" or the "desert" part of the inner life of present–day Man? It is not only the time when young people at school or college await their examination results but it can well be the season to re–examine our own ways and reach new resolves. Our teachers and houseparents can be heavily involved with self–examination when writing annual reports on each child and young person. Have I done enough to encourage his true potential and aims in life while seeing his difficulties; are we setting a helpful example of human self–development; was there a good mixture of sincerity and joy, exercise and art? Searching questions of self–knowledge may arise before we can go on holidays. These used to be "holy days," granted to us as a period of grace so that we might ready ourselves to take up new resolves and face new tests in life when autumn comes — after the 29th August which is traditionally the day of the beheading of John the Baptist whom Christ called the greatest among men born of a mother. Every summer St John may be experienced as the living example of that great human ideal: self–conscious selflessness.

Christmas and St John's tide, the solstices, can be seen as forming one beam of the cross of the seasons; Easter and the autumn festival of Michaelmas, the equinoxes, as the other. At Easter we turn to the festival of death and the renewal of life which since time immemorial have belonged to the existential and spiritual meaning of humankind and the

Earth. Our celebrations begin on Palm Sunday with following an old tradition of walking the boundaries of the parcel of land entrusted to our care. Among the little crowd there may be a child pushed in a wheelchair and another riding upright on horseback, and everyone is singing, re-joicing in spring and the beauty of fields and gardens with cows, horses and goats.

Holy Week is marked with work on the land preparing the ground and then coming to a climax on Good Friday with planting and sowing. This gives to the children a living experience of the meaning of Easter. Also in Holy Week, the adults perform plays about the mystery of Easter as reflected in human culture, past and present. On Easter Sunday the older children who have become fourteen in the course of the year attend their first "Youth Service" in the presence of parents and friends. They have been prepared in the preceding months for the step of leaving childhood and entering the "school of life" where they face their personal destiny. They may seek guidance and comfort in the living being of Christ, the power of love which is meaningful to all young people. In the afternoon of Easter Sunday, everyone scrambles out with fun and joy to hunt for the well-hidden Easter eggs. The Easter Hare has provided plentifully for big and small, and the day is completed with the satisfaction of "munching" chocolate eggs. The decorated real egg with its hidden yellow yolk speaks in a silent symbolic language of the power of the sun and the renewal of life.

The meaning of the Christian festivals, related to human suffering and joy, finds expression in a wealth of traditional and modern songs, such as:

> Forth he came at Easter, like the risen grain,
> he that for three days in the grave had lain,
> quick from the dead my risen Lord is seen:
> love is come again like wheat that springeth green.

These words belong to spring when the sap is rising in plants and trees and the forces of growth are again spread towards the sun. During aut-umn they withdraw again into the roots embedded in the earth. Our consciousness participates in the "breathing of nature": expanding and dreaming away to the heights of warmth and light in spring and summer, but contracting again in autumn and winter, supporting us to have a clear head and be alert in thinking and action, as the cold winds of autumn begin to blow. In the season of Michaelmas our children can be heard singing a new round:

St Micha—el, hero of the sun,
Give us your sword, the battle has begun.
Teach us to listen and to speak,
St Micha—el, hero of the sun.

The stories of the Archangel Michael and his earthly representative St George, fighting the dragon, speak deeply to the hearts of children and young people who have to battle with handicaps and deprivation. His sword is made of that light with which he can always outwit the devil whose devices are clever but evil. His name, Micha—el derives from the Hebrew *micha* meaning "who is like" and *el* meaning "God"; he is often depicted with the dragon underfoot while his gaze is directed straight ahead.

In preparation for Michaelmas Day, 29th September, we gather the harvest from our gardens and fields and each house community builds and decorates a harvest table. The festival stretches over three days during which we gather with the entire Community for a pageant and a festive harvest meal singing:

Micha—el, prince of angels,
Of fire is made your being
And wondrous is your beauty...

Another image shows Micha—el holding the scales weighing human souls who are crossing from life on Earth to life in the spirit. Rudolf Steiner held that the creation of a new Michaelmas festival would safeguard humankind's future. He spoke of Micha—el as the "Spirit of our Time" who leaves Man free and who works with the consequences of our actions. He promotes the ideal of modern Man: striving to do the good out of inner freedom.

The festival of Whitsun can be likened to the sun disc that surrounds the cross in the old Celtic designs. We have a tradition of celebrating it with a colourful King Arthur pageant, acting scenes of chivalry and religious devotion according to legends of King Arthur and his knights who used to gather around the Round Table at Whitsun. When they were assembled they expected a miracle to happen before the feast could begin. It provided an experience which gave each knight recognition and the reassurance needed to follow his individual quest for another year. We feel that celebrating Whitsun means to confirm the interdependence of the individual and the community. The Acts of the Apostles say: "When the day of Pentecost was fully come, they were all with one accord in one place." We, men of the present day, may live with the challenging question, can we be in accord with one another while following the quest of our own lives? Festivals are celebrated for our children as much as for the whole community and everywhere.

Experience has shown that our approach to religious life and celebrations is suitable for children and young people of different denominations and religions. A number of parents have expressed their appreciation that we take religious practice seriously and that their children have become more capable of joining their religious practices at home. Pupils who do not have such observances at home will retain the experience of a school which fosters their inner life and their sense of human values in a world that thirsts for them.

# 4 An holistic view of child development

Rudolf Steiner took the idea of evolution, referred to in Chapter 2, a step further by making us aware of the parallel between child development and the historic development of humankind. The evolution and development of human consciousness since before the time of early cultures up to the present has gone through distinct stages and the growing child repeats them in some aspects. In other words, the evolution of the species (phylogeny) and of Man's cultural development are recapitulated in the evolution of the individual child's maturation (ontogeny). The mythological age of humankind had its own great cultures, which were as different from ours as the young child's mind is from that of the adult of the present time. Our overall curriculum and, in particular, our classroom syllabus seek to respond to these stages of maturation. An outline and several examples of the latter (the Waldorf School curriculum, which for the purposes of this book, we call our classroom syllabus) are included in Chapter 5. First an account is given of the purposes of learning in general and then a description of the three phases of infancy, childhood and adolescence.

## Learning in general

Learning is part of daily life: the younger we are the greater is our capacity for learning, the older we grow the more learning can be enriched by experience and transformed into ability and, in later life, learning and experience may deepen into wisdom. A young child relates to his environment with intense powers of imitation and these lead him, with his vivid and creative imagination, to develop moral values which will be deeply felt and strongly held throughout his life. These values will come to expression in his language, his way of thinking, in his practical and social skills. As the foundations of morality are laid in the first five to seven years of life, it is helpful when any efforts in educating young children are conducted by way of imagination and play. It is, of course, possible to give children intellectual training at a very early stage, but good and evil play no part in intellectual pursuits. Premature intellectual training can deprive a child of a most important part of his childhood, impairing his later development. It may then be almost impossible to redress the resulting imbalance. When the child reaches the second dentition he is ready to learn about the world through the guidance of his teachers and parents whose authority he loves and trusts. This requires teachers and parents to accompany the development of the child with tact and a sustained enthusiasm to introduce him to the magnificence and beauty of the world. The experience of beauty in every subject taught is of major importance for the wellbeing of a child in Lower and Middle School. Only when the child reaches adolescence is he ready to respond to purely intellectual truth without losing his sense of morality and his aesthetic appreciation. For those of our pupils who are intellectually less gifted it is helpful if in adolescence they are introduced to practical work, in the quality of which truth can also be experienced. Simultaneously, all older pupils need this new intellectual emphasis to be balanced by continuing practice in art, music, poetry and various practical skills.

# The stage of infancy

The human child arrives on Earth imbued with a primal trust in the world, helpless and dependent on the love and care of his parents. His senses are truly open to everything that meets him and he has life forces which are ready to last for probably seventy years or more. At first he has a "peripheral consciousness" and looks at his body from outside, especially through the eyes of his mother. The wonder of his first smile is then the heavenly dawning of the individuality about to take up his abode in his body, his own "house." In the process of contracting his wide awareness into a centred Ego–consciousness which is aware of itself and a vantage from which to survey the world, the young child has a relationship to his natural and human environment which can be compared to an adult's religious relationship to and longing for the Divine Spirit. The child's "blood circulation, breathing and its digestive proces- ses adore its environment" (Rudolf Steiner). Therefore our task, with respect to him, has a priestly nature but we guide him into a life of earthly nature, whereas a priest guides us into spiritual life.

An awareness of this belongs to the great task of parenthood. A heal- thy young child naturally and eagerly imitates what is around him. We, who are part of his environment, should therefore feel called upon to conduct our lives in the awareness that our experiences, emotions and thoughts deeply influence the child and that they even work into the living processes of his body. Our habits, our ways of walking and our manner of speaking, our most subtle movements as well as the home environment which we create, all directly influence the child's habits and health, laying for him a lifetime foundation of attitudes and human values. The child craves for the grace of his environment as we crave for the grace of God. We could not carry this responsibility were it not for the love streaming from the child towards us and to which we can res- pond. The nature of the relationship between parent and child is of quite a different quality from that between other intimate friends. He needs nothing less than the unconditional love of his parents and they in turn must not be asked to be impartial towards him. In the first months and years mother is usually the all-important anchor whose presence gives stability and security to life. From her the child begins to learn the mother tongue which will be a vehicle of meaning for life; to learn about the "do's and don'ts" of life, and about both direct and imponderable relationships to other people, relatives, friends and visitors. The actions and movements of mother in her daily tasks exert a directly, formative influence on the child. "That's how mummy does it" is implicit in her child's beholding and imitation. Mother's moodiness or her equanimity strongly affect the environment and experiences her child has.

Learning, in the early years, has an almost unlimited potential but its realization can be limited by home circumstances. What the child sees and experiences, especially of human activity, such as ordered move- ments of work, makes its mark. If, as young children, we have watched "men at work" with all the intensity that children have it is so much easier to learn the movements and skills pertaining to work when the time comes for us to become responsible for our own activities. Young children are often seen to imitate their father's walk or his way of talking to people or his mannerisms. A father has a strong influence on his child who is learning to master the body which does not yet know how to do things. Learning to stand, to take a step and to utter increasingly mean-ingful sounds, and then to co–ordinate these meanings with own percepts and thoughts, is in all a marvel of co–ordination and learning, of mastery of our human frame. Together these embody a complex process of learn-ing neither paralleled nor equalled at any other time of life. All this is tacit and incidental learning not consciously directed by the child, yet eagerly *absorbed* and *imitated* in these first years. The capacity for tacit learning diminishes as we grow up but it can still play a very useful part in educational and therapeutic work with older children who have devel-opmental handicaps and is further referred to in later chapters.

Sensory overstimulation and direct "feeding in" of information are among the greatest dangers of our time for young children before the second dentition. The golden rule for parents of young children should be: direct your actions and your sense perception, your emotions and your thoughts as you would like to have them echoed and live on in your children, and provide a healthy and ordered home environment in which they can feel free to play. The play of a young child is a serious activity; in playing, he responds to the world and re–creates it in his own personal way. Therefore, a good toy leaves room for the child's imagination to work. A simple rag doll, soft and welcoming, can in the child's imagin-ation become mother, little sister, princess or nurse while the so–called "perfect" plastic doll offers little inspiration but rather creates a grey world of sameness. Too much viewing of television can condemn a child to passive participation, paralysing potential powers of creativity. By the same token, the use of computer software, which is programmed artificial intelligence, may whip up pointless emotions at the expense of creativity and social contact. As the child grows up his play activity goes to sleep, as it were. When he is adult it awakens as inner creative strength and the ability to take his life in hand. The tendency among young adults of our time towards aimlessness, isolation and feeling restless or uncomfortable within themselves may be the result of lack of adequate play in infancy and childhood. This lack may be due to an unfortunate childhood environment or a failure in a child's development or both: the child who does not play has a reduced chance to master his destiny in adulthood.

# The stage of childhood

When a child reaches the time of second dentition his *Gestalt,* his whole form, is different from that of the infant and toddler and he is ready to go to school and begin functional learning, which is to say that he becomes *aware* that he is learning. If functional learning is introduced at an earlier age it does not increase a child's intelligence but it does interfere with the development of that child's creative powers. The phase of play described in the previous section, is then curtailed and he is deprived of an essential part of his resources in life. Some possible consequences of this deprivation are reduced motivation in early adulthood, neurotic behaviour, lassitude, or a general lack of "life force," leading to physical frailty. In the course of the first five to seven years a child assumes command of his body, and nature renews every living cell in it which culminates in shedding his first teeth; then he has made his "earthly house" his own.

A child naturally looks up to his teacher as the authority who shows him how to do things and teaches him to understand the world. He, therefore, meets the teacher with great expectations. The child wants to work for his teacher and enjoys learning about the beauty, the truth and the goodness of the world. He is ready to extend his love and trust provided this is reciprocated by the teacher's love and faith in each young pupil. The creative powers with which he has imitated the world even into the organic processes of his body, and which are the wellspring of his play, can now be transformed into powers of directed learning. Static and purely intellectual concepts given to the young pupil in the first years of school can become oppressive to him, like a pair of shoes which are becoming too small: he needs living concepts which can develop and grow with him as his mind unfolds. These can be given to him when all school subjects are taught in an artistic and rhythmical way, when the teacher tries to let the world shine into the classroom through the medium of movement, singing and reciting, painting and drawing, modelling and making things. This enlivens the necessary conceptual content of lessons. The child of this age is artistic by nature and responds to such an approach. The Rudolf Steiner syllabus, which is used in Waldorf Schools, takes account of this. It is broadly based and responds to the stages of child development thereby furthering and allowing for the maturation of the whole child. Language development is fostered throughout all the years of schooling; writing, reading and mathematics are introduced to the class at the appropriate stages and are then subject to individual and small group teaching programmes according to the individual special needs of our pupils.

Eileen Hutchins, a pioneer of Waldorf education in Britain, said that each subject needs to be introduced at the moment when the unfolding powers of the child are ready to receive it, and it is only the laws of the child's own nature which can determine what subjects should be learned at what age.[11] Thus the syllabus needs to be considered in its entirety. Subjects are introduced stage by stage so that they interrelate with one another, and after completion of the twelve classes, the many themes, as they recur at intervals through school life, must be brought together to form a kind of world harmony.

The syllabus cannot in any way be dogmatic. Education is an art and, out of the interplay of personality between teacher and class, knowledge is forever found anew. While fundamentally the development of the child follows certain definite trends, in every country and in every school teachers have to find the way of approach fitted to the requirements and dispositions of their particular groups of children. Further, we have to take into account the balance between those subjects which primarily call forth the activity in thinking; those which give expression and form to the life of emotion and feeling; those which demand practical ability and strengthen and develop motivation and will. Above all we have to guide the pupil in the development of these mental or soul powers so that as he reaches adult life he can become master of himself.

In the first years of the child's school life, it is the task of the class teacher to link together all the different subjects. She accompanies her children for the first eight years in school so that the "world picture," which she forms for them, may be consistently developed. Thus a real understanding and confidence develop between teacher and pupils; from this springs the authority and true discipline that children of this age so much require.

The *six-to-seven-year-old* is still intimately connected to both his human and natural environment; he does not yet experience himself as being totally separated from his surroundings. He experiences self especially through the rhythm of breathing and blood circulation and, therefore, he has a natural relationship to everything expressed in rhyme, rhythm and beat. This stage of being corresponds to the mythological age of humankind, as expressed in classical fairy tales. The characters of these fairy tales are archetypes which speak directly to the young child's imagination and the child finds great satisfaction and joy in living with the pictures contained in fairy tales and relates intimately to them. The elements of writing and reading can be introduced through stories and images.

The *seven–to–eight–year–old* child's rough and tumble games are coupled with a first measure of detachment. He becomes clearer in thought, more aware of his playmates as separate individuals but the elements of nature in his immediate environment still speak to him and to one another with a human voice. Animal fables reflect this development and stories of "good people" (especially the saints) appeal to the eight–year–old's emerging sense of goodness. The fables and timeless stories of saints give him the same joy and feeling of satisfaction that he had the previous year when living with the images of the fairy tales.

When the child becomes *nine years old,* he undergoes quite a marked change. He becomes noticeably more self–conscious and stronger. A further step is taken in separating self from environment: where previously he felt generally more at one with the people and things around him, and therefore took them for granted, he now increasingly feels himself separated from his environment. He begins to doubt and question the familiar things and people that surround him, no longer taking everything for granted. This is a critical time in child development, when the child needs security and reassurance, therefore the nine–year–old makes great claim on the wisdom and tact of the teacher. It is a stage of child development reflected in the biblical story of the fall from paradise, which with other stories from the Old Testament and their authoritative divine justice, give the child a great sense of security. Studying the archetypal human occupations, such as farming and building, reassures the child that there is meaning to his own life and that of the adult world into which he will grow.

The *nine–to–ten–year–old* child is entering the golden heart of childhood when there is, hopefully, a good balance between play and work, imagination and thought. By studying Norse mythology the child can once again experience the joy and satisfaction that was brought at a younger stage by the fairy tales and then by the fables and stories of saints. The *ten–year–old* has an awakening interest in the world and this is nurtured by a study of animals and of local geography.

When he grows to *eleven years of age* the child reaches a certain harmony. His body form has the beautifully balanced proportions of Greek art. Balance between play and work, imagination and thought, represents the calm before the first warnings of the storm of puberty — and a study of the classical Greek culture fits with the eleven–year–old's sense of harmony and balance. This is the time of transition from the mythologies to history. The child's continued interest in the world is deepened by a study of plants, their form and structure appealing to the child's sense of harmony and beauty.

By the age of *twelve years* the child begins to lose his natural grace and harmony. The body loses its perfect proportions, movements become angular, even slightly jerky. The child experiences himself through the growing bones of his skeleton and has, therefore, a ready grasp of mechanics and of the relationship of cause and effect. He is ready to be introduced to physics as the first science subject. Geometry, because of its mechanical construction, appeals to the twelve–year–old, and through it a relationship to harmony and beauty, which came so naturally to the eleven–year–old, can be retained and further developed. Twelve–year–old children have a great sense of personal justice and of right and wrong though often there is a struggle with the latter at this age. Historically this is expressed in the culture of Ancient Rome.

On reaching *thirteen years of age* a child is at a stage of maturity where he is able to distinguish clearly between his inner experience and his awareness of the world in which he lives. In school he can become adaptable and a clarity of thought develops. With the onset of puberty the mind opens out and the thirteen–year–old seeks to explore his world to the full, both within and outside the classroom. This can, indeed, be a traumatic time; limits of behaviour are tested and need to be re-established. The teacher needs to be firm and wise but above all must feed the child's enquiring mind. This stage of child development corresponds to the Renaissance when the discoveries in science and art and the explorations of the globe took place. These form the core of the curriculum for this year and chemistry is added as a second science.

By the time the child reaches *the age of fourteen,* the transition from childhood to youth has taken place. With puberty the youth enters the final stage of the physiological maturing process. The adolescent begins to shape his own life, in school his adaptability increases, he becomes dependable and develops a sense of duty. This can be a time of consolidation and reflection, of looking back to childhood and on to the future. The adolescent becomes self–critical and critical of others, while at the same time he looks for people and historical characters he can model himself on and idealize. With his increasing powers of logical thought and rationalization the adolescent has to meet the full impact of modern intellectual thought and achievements. A study of the three great revolutions, the French Revolution, the Industrial and the Agricultural Revolutions can lead the thirteen–to–fourteen–year old to a first appreciation of the complexity of modern life. Anatomy as a first biological study is now added to the sciences. These are the final stages through which the class teacher, who has accompanied the child from the age of seven through to fourteen, guides her class. In the next class a different approach is required.

Such a conception sees the physical, emotional and mental phases of development in their harmony. However, these three aspects can be out of step and this may cause disruption and special needs in the individual child. The Waldorf syllabus, as part of our overall curriculum, furthers and restores harmony between body, mind and spirit, and is the strongest educational healing element we can apply. It is suitable for all pupils: those who are of average developmental standards, those who are brilliant and those who have special needs. Forty years ago (in 1950) under the guidance of Karl König we introduced this curriculum to all children in Camphill.

Our experience has borne out that those who have severe impairments also benefit from the Waldorf Syllabus. This benefit is enhanced when they can participate for part of the day in a class, as well as share life in a family unit with others who have different needs and are both intellectually and emotionally on other levels. In a class of pupils with different impairments, each child has something to give to the other. Some who cannot demonstrate through speech and action what they have learned, may absorb through shared experience much of the curriculum presented and often they become of social value to the class and in the wider context. Thereby, healing processes take place and social situations are created which further the maturation of the pupils and help them to participate in the activities of the class as well as to take in the content presented. It is also a social deed to include everyone into the body of historical, cultural development and not to leave them high and dry with nothing to relate to. The teacher in a Rudolf Steiner School for children with special needs takes regard of this and will usually, for the first part of the school morning, approach the class as children of one age group, who under her guidance, can complement and balance each other. They are primarily children of a certain chronological age and, whatever handicap they may have to cope with, they subconsciously expect the teacher standing in front of them to introduce them to the splendour and glory of the world. They expect to be taught all the things which the adults know and can do. Our approach means that each child participates in a balanced programme of group teaching and individual tuition. His participation in a class of children of his chronological age group, who are addressed according to their age, supports his maturation and dignity. His basic skills, of writing, reading and mathematics is furthered in small ability groups or in individual lessons. These are arranged by the class teacher who accompanies her children for many years and knows their individual needs. In addition to this, special therapies, such as music therapy or curative eurythmy, may be prescribed to individuals in consultation with the Schools' doctors.

We try never to be rigid in our arrangements and exceptions to the rule are discussed in case conferences together with the Schools' doctors. A child who is both mentally and physically very immature, for example, may begin to grow and thrive when he is permitted to participate in a class of children who, by and large, are his size and at his stage of physical and emotional development though chronologically younger. A child newly admitted to our Schools who has a fear of attending school can benefit from a period without formal schooling until he wants to join an activity he realizes that the other children enjoy. Further, we have small highly specialized classes for children with multiple handicaps who are deaf and/or aphasic or who are so severely disturbed that they cannot benefit from participating in one of the other classes. In each case it is important not to lose sight either of the child's actual chronological age, or of the necessary inner attitude to him and his human dignity.


# Adolescence and independence

In adolescence we experience phases of alienation and doubt in order to attain "earthly maturity" as Rudolf Steiner calls it. Based on this earthly maturity we can gain our personal freedom, find our own friends, develop our individual aims in life — a process which takes another seven years and sometimes much longer. In the period of this transition from being sheltered in the haven of childhood, to being exposed to the open seas of life, we are bound to be uncertain and vulnerable. We may appear physically strong and mature, we may be intellectually clever but we lack the wisdom and inner certainty which can only grow with life's experience.

So we are particularly exposed to the great danger of our present civilization which manifests as the splitting of the personality into three parts: the individual's intellect, his emotional life, and motivations on which his actions are based. These three can lose touch with each other and the result is that the individual's humanity is lost. This danger is enhanced by the overemphasis which our present civilization places on the development of intellectual power on the one hand and sexual prowess on the other. The former is supported by parents and teachers who hold on firmly to those present day educational convictions which expect the adolescent to devote himself to purely functional and intellectual learning and pass his exams. Sadly the adolescents' sexual maturation is being exploited by whole industries for which an adolescent subculture is good business (and the victims become ever younger) and by adults who may lack fulfilment in their own lives. The young person may revolt against this onslaught on his integrity for at heart he searches for a meaningful life conducted by people who have ideals and are true to themselves.

We endeavour to support the adolescent in our home life and in his own social life to find opportunities which can satisfy his sense of adventure and his wish to explore the world. We try to balance this with challenges to help develop his sense of responsibility. He needs loving and sometimes assured guidance to become aware of the consequences of his own actions before he can take responsibility for others. It is then natural for him to search for truth in the world and it may be very disturbing when he discovers the dishonesty which can be found in society. Such disappointments and the consequent anxiety, depression or urge for "revenge" and destruction can be overcome if we succeed in fostering his love for the world and for the humanity in each person. It helps him to appreciate truth in depth and to develop motivation to strive to do the good in the world.

In the classroom an artistic education offers the ideal remedy to balance the necessary functional, intellectual and practical learning because it involves the whole human being with his motivational, emotional and intellectual powers. Therefore all scientific as well as practical subjects are presented with an element of art in the teaching method, and the actual practice of the visual arts, music and eurythmy continues right through the Upper School. From the fifteenth year onwards the young person's level of maturation necessitates that the different subjects be presented by specialist teachers. The time of Lower and Middle School, when the child's natural tendency was towards accepting whatever his teacher called beautiful or ugly, good or bad, true or false is over. The adolescent wants to judge and decide these for himself. However, fifteen- and sixteen–year–olds with special needs still require a teacher or class guardian who knows them well and in whom they can trust. He can give them a sense of security which they need as their emotional development is often delayed. At the same time, the encounter with more specialist teachers gives the pupil a broader scope on which to model himself.

In his *fifteenth year,* the young person's spirit of independence grows. He tends to become taciturn and inwardly taken up with his emotions, and may outwardly appear indifferent but he is at the same time growing very perceptive. His strong emotional awareness of inner life can find a helpful expression in personal hobbies and his aspirations can be guided through hearing biographies of great personalities. The subjects of the syllabus call for active emotional involvement and simultaneously use the rising intellectual ability in a healthy way. They take the young person away from self–concern and guide him to use his new mental and physical powers better to grasp the nature of the world, and to become part of it for the benefit of other people.

History of the recent centuries is looked at again with the question in mind: "What stirred in people as their ideals and impulses?"; for example: "What prompted Robert Falcon Scott and Roald Amundsen to strive to reach the South Pole?" The young person studies the enquiring mind of the inventor, who as a single individual may have changed the social situation throughout the world. Such individuals invented the mechanical loom, the steam engine, the motor car, the aeroplane, dynamite, and so on. This historic development can be further elucidated by questions such as: "What stirred in the mind of the composer Mozart when he wrote *The Magic Flute* at the same time as these inventions began?"

History of art, especially of painting and sculpture from the ancient Egyptian culture to the late Renaissance, fosters the appreciation of aesthetic values and ideals of beauty and an awareness of their development. Such studies, conducted in the course of this and the following year, give the young person the possibility of finding his own favourite style, be it Egyptian art, El Greco, or a modern painter. A study of humour and comedy in literature at the time when the adolescent feels a little raw and vulnerable helps him to become more detached.

The young person in his *sixteenth year* often becomes even more engrossed in self–awareness and the influence of his peer group becomes very important to him. We therefore endeavour to increase his interest in the world and in all aspects of humanity. His natural and urgent concern about the future, both his own and that of humankind, can provide a good motivation. The syllabus lays emphasis on appreciation of poetry and drama, thereby offering creative ways of self–expression and self education. History of art continues with the great masters of painting from Rembrandt's time to the present day. In history lessons he looks back at the cultural heritage of ancient times and learns to appreciate its impulse and its impact on the twentieth century. Questions can be raised such as: "What is the message of Hellas for our modern age?" "Does ancient Indian culture affect people in our own time?" Another study period turns to the earth as an organism, raising the awareness of ecological and environmental responsibility. The teaching of technology and practical skills is a growing task with this age group. We foster the development of skills required to transform natural materials into articles which are both useful and beautiful.

As he reaches *seventeen years of age,* the young person's spirit of independence becomes less impulsive and questions arise concerning the meaning of life and the role of the individual. Great inspiration can now be given to him through a study and appreciation of music and its development. The same holds good for the study of literature such as the stories of Parsifal illustrating personal failure and fulfilment. Biology as a key subject in the syllabus for this age group now pays special attention to the observation, with the help of a microscope, of the tension between chaos and form in developing organisms. A counterbalance to these pursuits is the study of the universe with the help of a telescope. Experience gained in these scientific pursuits can be related to learning about the individual and society. Technology as an application of scientific knowledge in everyday life is also studied.

The education of the *eighteen–year–old* is used to guide his integration into our present day society and cultural heritage, help him to face his own responsibilities and work with commitment. The previous studies of visual arts, poetry, drama and music now find a synthesis and continuation in learning about architecture which can then be understood as technology as well as an artistic expression of human, social and religious attitudes. In history, we review the different cultures, and their influence upon each other and on our present time is appreciated. The studies of biology in this year present a survey of the animal and plant kingdom in their natural order and relationship, from the lowest to the most advanced organisms. The young person is guided to live with a compassionate relationship to the natural world. The study of technology and sciences which was started in the past year continues.

Our syllabus for adolescents sees every subject as related to Man. Science, art and religion are not treated as objective "authorities" but are placed in the human context. At the beginning of adolescence the young person has reached the most "physical" phase of his development which includes sexual maturation. In many ways he is then liable to feel "thrown out of the nest" and isolated. His education aims to establish him as an individual and lead him towards independence. This would enable him to act out of his sense of duty where duty arises from his own motivation and wish to do the good; a maxim which Goethe expressed in the aphorism: "Duty is loving the deed which we have demanded of ourselves." The young person can then at the end of his years at school see his place in human society in a further perspective. This holds good for young people who have special needs just as much as it does for those who are more intellectually or socially gifted. As described in the previous chapter, this syllabus is helpful to any young person and can be therapeutic to those whose mental, emotional and/or physical development is retarded, disturbed or out of balance. In the last three years of schooling with us the emphasis gradually shifts towards the practical application of skills and of the intelligence needed in working with various crafts. We continue in a practical and artistic way to make available to them the range of subjects in our syllabus. In the final year they can gain work experience as will be described in the final section of the next chapter, Classes 11, 12 and beyond.

# 5 Education in the classroom

## The rhythm of teaching and memory

The subjects of the school syllabus which embrace a definite content and are taught in a fundamentally artistic way in Rudolf Steiner Schools are presented in the first part of the morning, each day, in blocks of three to five weeks. To these subjects belong all the humanities and sciences, and they include elements of language, music, movement and art. Other subjects which require rhythmical repetition in order to acquire certain skills are taken daily, with pupils who have special needs, in small remedial groups or individually. To these belong literacy, numeracy and language as well as remedial movement and pre–reading exercises.

This approach to education is well described by A.C. Harwood, Waldorf teacher, writer and poet.[12] He said that something which is only known by the head is not even half–known. A real *feeling* for the subject must be developed and this is always a matter of time. Feeling, however, especially in childhood, wants to find expression. This can be attained when we learn to recite what some of the poets have felt and written about the matter in hand; when we paint pictures, model, make compositions or act little plays, using our artistic and creative powers to penetrate more deeply into the subject. In doing this we are also calling upon the powers of will. Thereby all the faculties of the human being become engaged in a way not possible unless a stretch of time is devoted to the subject.

The objective of learning is not necessarily to remember. It may even be salutary to forget. It is only when we forget the early pains and struggles of forming letters that we acquire the capacity for writing. The adult does not remember all the history he learned but he may hope to have acquired a standard of character and conduct, a sense of affairs and a feeling of change and development in culture. Naturally there is no-thing against having a well–stocked mind provided it does not prevent the development of other capacities. But it is still more important to allow knowledge to sink into one in such a way that it becomes fruitful for life; this is best done when we *feel* deeply all that we learn. For the life of feeling is less conscious, more dream–like, than intellectual acti-vity and leads to the subconscious life of will where the deep creative capacities of Man have their being. It is from this sphere that knowledge can emerge again as something deeply significant for life. It is not what we remember exactly, but what we transform which is of real value to our lives. In this transformation the process of forgetting, of allowing subjects to sink into the unconscious before "re–membering" them is an important element. Similarly, though relating to a much shorter span of time, Rudolf Steiner education has regard to the manner in which the actual sleep life of children should be brought into connection with the process of memorizing. Children should not be questioned about what they have just been told, to see if they have been attentive because this calls for and produces only the most superficial memory. They should first be allowed to sleep on what they have learned. On the next day they can recount it and it will probably already be enriched by the less con-scious powers of their being. Only on the third day when they have twice taken it into their sleep, should they discuss what they have learned, giving their own opinions, producing comparisons and illustrations. Such an education encourages that deeper reflection in which the whole Man is involved. But it is only possible where teaching takes place in such a regular daily sequence as the block periods provide.

Our way of teaching requires careful planning and continuous reassess-ment but it cannot be determined by programming and testing. The teacher endeavours to create an atmosphere of enthusiasm in the class for each subject presented. This enthusiasm supports the pupil in applying himself and realizing that he is learning. At the same time it fosters tacit and incidental learning especially for those who have severe learning difficulties. In our classes the time spent on the more intellectual aspects of learning may have to be shortened and accordingly the artistic and creative part of the daily block period can be expanded. This allows the individual pupil to absorb in his own way as much of each subject as he can. Each pupil has his preferred subjects: some "shine" more when it comes to practical application, some are better at artistic work or at singing, others can remember well and help the class recall what they have heard and experienced. We know of children who "give back" nothing at all of what they have actually taken in and digested until a whole year has passed and a subject is taken up again in another block period. We have even encountered pupils suffering from autism who, for many years, were unable to show any direct response in class until in adolescence they felt ready to do so and suddenly showed that they could read and write and remember much of what they had heard in class. Those of our older pupils who have emotional and behavioural difficulties will, as a rule, make great efforts not to miss classes because they appreciate the syllabus and enjoy their lessons. Our way of educating children and young people does not imprint cold facts and mere codes of behaviour into their minds but it aims to guide them towards a true understanding of the world, enriched by their own imagination. It helps them to relate to their environment and to other people with human understanding and it lays foundations which allow young people and adults to develop their own individual powers of motivation.

# Artistic education and aesthetic experience

We consider aesthetic experiences to be an integral part of our overall curriculum and our classroom syllabus. Lessons in visual arts, music and eurythmy are taken throughout the years of school; they are not an option or "icing on the cake." They provide the necessary balance to the more academic pursuits and the training of skills; they are essential to the learning and maturation process. Through practising art work, we educate the whole being of the child; he becomes deeply involved and interested emotionally, his creative abilities and strength of will are fostered, his attention span is extended, his powers of observation and judgment are sharpened. Many skills requiring sensory and manual co-ordination are practised, as this happens at the same time. Art is not merely a way of self–expression or self–indulgence, it is also a discipline and some of its techniques must be learned before a degree of self-expression can be achieved. Lessons in aesthetics are structured in correspondence with our developmental approach and creative work develops as and when a skill has been developed. Even more fundamentally it is a feature of our syllabus that there should be no formal lesson which does not contain an element of art. Learning objectives for classes as well as for individual children require at all times to be complemented by aesthetic experiences. In fact, lessons are most successful if these objectives include such experiences. We may see the functional learning aspect related to a process of "inhaling" and the aesthetic activity as the necessary complement of "exhaling."

Another aspect of artistic education is the aesthetic experiences — or the lack thereof — provided by the environment in which we live. We as curative teachers, try to penetrate our surroundings with an artistic quality and, by our own efforts, to create beauty and harmony. The teachers draw their own pictures on the board and thereby stimulate the creativity of their children. The teachers' and children's drawings and paintings, with all their shortcomings, are of more value to the class than any posters because they have been involved in the creative process of making them. In addition to this, well chosen modern paintings and prints of old masters surround us in all rooms, just as the works of nature surround us when we are in a garden or in a beautiful landscape. So we seek to create harmony and balance for those who live and work in these rooms. The architectural design of classrooms and dwelling–houses is an expression of the spirit which is at work in the place where these buildings stand. It has a deep influence on the attitudes, the wellbeing and even the morality of those who live and work there, and children and growing young people are even more affected by it than adults who are more set in their ways. We are fortunate enough to have our own architects, who design beautiful organic forms to express something of the purpose of a building, its rooms and its furniture. Such forms are not merely aesthetic but, when well used, are practical and effective too. In a classroom they engender an atmosphere of concentration and work; in a dwelling–house, of comfort and feeling at home; in an assembly hall, of shelter for large as well as small gatherings, for intimate as well as festive occasions. Warm colours are helpful in rooms used for younger children and the cooler shades are better for adolescents. The use of varnished wood panelling on some of the walls and ceilings gives a living quality to any room and is also very practical. Good architecture and interior design, well maintained, create a sense of value and appreciation for the environment in which we live. It instils a caring attitude into children and young people which becomes a quality for life.

# Eurythmy

Eurythmy is an art form based on the archetypal movements inherent in human speech and music. Eurythmy allows speech and music to become visible.[13]

In speech eurythmy, the movements done to accompany a poem or prose narrative come from the actual vowels and consonants that are heard, so that when the sound "a" occurs then the appropriate gesture is done to accompany it and so on throughout the poem. The vowels reveal the inner soul quality of the human being and his corresponding language. The consonants express the activity or processes in nature herself. The meaning of the poem can be interpreted through moving in different directions over various forms, either strictly geometrical or freely obeying the grammatical rules of the language's structure. The combination of movement and gesture then corresponds to the feelings within the poem, creating a quality of colour and mood, dynamic and force to bring the sounds alive. The concept or thought behind each word can then also become visible. All this is artistically interpreted by the performing eurythmist to express in a wonderfully weaving and all–encompassing texture a visible experience and perception of the spoken word.

Eurythmy done to musical composition, or tone eurythmy, is creating visible song. The different elements of music are made visible through the human body. Each tone has a corresponding gesture as does each interval between the tones, experienced through the bone structure of the arms and hands. The elements of music are related also to the dimension of space: the pitch moving through different ranges between high and low, the melody flowing quickly or slowly forwards or backwards, the rhythm steadily providing the impetus in time and the beat holding strict balance between right and left. The eurythmist brings the musical elements into life and movement. The inherent laws and structures of music begin to sound forth, to sing.

The gestures of eurythmy are not simply symbols which represent processes but are developed from the archetypal movements Man makes to accompany these processes in himself. Because of this, watching a performance of eurythmy or carrying out the movements, can call up powerfully the mood of what is being expressed without it being necessary to understand what is done. As with all forms of art, eurythmy speaks directly to the feelings of Man.

There are numerous ways in which eurythmy is uniquely helpful in education. Besides being in itself an artistic medium through which children can enjoy expressing themselves, eurythmy develops in them a strong feeling for an understanding of music and poetry. In language study eurythmy can offer an appealing approach to grammar, as all aspects of speech can be differentiated in movement in a way that involves the child's feelings and interest, requiring precision without being dry or abstract.

In doing eurythmy a healthy unity of thought, feeling and movement is developed together with an ability to orientate and move in space, singly and in close co–operation with others. By performing the eurythmy to suitable music or a poem, the exercises remain in the form of art and play whilst allowing the child or young person to explore and rehearse social activity. In this way eurythmy develops the principle embodied in many children's ring games and in the dramatic acting often done with young people. However, to the extent that the eurythmy gestures are artistically carried out, the inner processes are fully engaged and the situation enacted becomes a real experience for the pupil.

# Academic subjects

This section presents a few examples of the syllabus referred to in the chapter on child development: the teaching of geography, history, chemistry, English and number as developed throughout the years at school. It will be followed by examples of the curriculum for three different age groups including art, crafts and work training. Again we wish to ask the reader to be aware that the syllabus is used as an educational measure to support the *whole* person with due regard to his emotional, mental and physical development, and his social integration and maturation. The teacher may present a subject to the whole class for a brief ten minutes or dwell on it for a longer period of time. She may then use the content for artistic or practical activities with the class and individual pupils as needed. It is intrinsic to this approach that the lessons arise always anew out of the interaction between the teacher and her pupils and the class as a whole.

## The geography syllabus

In Classes 1 and 2 (age 6–8) nature stories, taking examples from the immediate environment of the child are told, painted, acted and brought to life in his soul, kindling a loving awareness for that which is unconsciously familiar.

In Class 3 (age 8–9), the area studied is widened as tradesmen, craftsmen, farmers and fishermen of the locality are visited and observed at work. The class then takes up some practical project involving the use of tools. The discipline of practical skills is experienced. By working together in co-operation a moral experience of interdependence is fostered.

In Class 4 (age 9–10), the local area is a central study. Determined by the physical features, the historic growth of human activity can be followed, leading to an understanding of the present situation. Industries of town and country and landmarks of history are visited. Those children whose understanding is very limited can, nevertheless, be guided to have an experience of a local community with its roots and traditions which supports the child's sense of identity.

As the child grows up through Class 5 (age 10–11), he is led further afield to the geography of his own country. The configuration of the land, the economic conditions, trade and industry are studied. The awareness of the reality of industrial and human interdependence among those who live far away from each other should awaken a sense of brotherliness. This can be supported by, for example, modelling a landscape and imagining or acting the lives of those who were involved in the making of the chairs and desks which are used in the classroom.

When in Class 6 the children become twelve, we can continue drawing and painting geographical maps and reliefs, which adds an artistic element to the lessons and can involve every pupil. In this way our study can be widened to a general survey of the continent of Europe followed by studies of climatic, cultural and economic conditions in chosen European countries. The most varied, as well as the most typical, of European situations can be presented: Norway contrasted with Spain, land–locked Switzerland with seafaring Holland would be good examples; France and Germany show an all round picture of a European industrial country. In this wider context also a study of the phases of the moon and the movements of the Sun and Earth is undertaken. Again every pupil can be involved in plays and games in which imaginary journeys are acted.

At the beginning of adolescence in Class 7 (age 12–13), the approach taken in the previous two years is expanded to cover other continents. Tropical Africa and the Polar regions show the climatic extremes of earthly life and cultural adaptation. The zodiac and other main constellations can become familiar in relation to the movements of the Earth. Our pupils will now have gained an experience of north and south and in many a first understanding for the dimensions of the globe is dawning.

In Class 8 (age 13–14), this will be followed by an east–west study. The challenges arising out of present–day Western economy meeting the older civilizations in the East can be examined and imaginatively portrayed. The American continent, north and south presenting countries of varying climatic conditions and different stages of development, can conclude a first geographical world survey.

In the Upper School, beginning with Class 9 (age 14–15), through artistic and practical activities all pupils can be helped to have a feeling for the Earth as an ecological organism. Bearing this in mind, the teacher introduces the young person to physical geography. An important aspect of this is the discovery of the cross formed by the chief mountain ranges, north–south in the Americas and west–east from the Pyrenees and Alps across the Caucasus to the Himalayas.

In Class 10 (age 15–16), the movement of water, air and warmth on and around the Earth and its effect can be studied. Prevailing winds, tides and ocean currents, glaciers, animal and bird migration can be presented and acted to build a picture of the living Earth so that a feeling of responsibility for ecology can grow in the individual young person.

At the beginning of Classes 11 and 12 (age 16–18), the pupils have a practical course in basic surveying and in orienteering. This is followed by drawing maps and the study of ordnance survey, political and topographical world maps. Looking at techniques of map making from ancient times to satellite surveys provides another source of combining learning with practical and artistic work. In the final year of school the syllabus turns to three aspects of Man's existence: Man living with Man, Man's living with the Earth and its resources, Man's spiritual beliefs and its manifestations. The spiritual and ideological backgrounds which influence nations and their inter–relationships can be studied. In this light, social forms and political motivation can be looked at and a sense for world trade and commerce in relation to resources and needs can be awakened. Finally a feeling for ecological responsibilities can be stimulated by an attempt to survey the attitudes of different nations.

## The history syllabus

In the history syllabus, the practical implication of the idea that the child and young person in their development repeat aspects of the historic development of humankind from the most distant past to our present time is most apparent. In the first classes (age 6–9), the history syllabus provides story contents which are related daily at a regular time of the school morning. Here again the artistic creativity of the teacher is called upon: while telling the story she may use glove puppets to support those children who lack word understanding and could otherwise not follow. Singing and acting plays, poems and rhymes written or adapted for the class, are needed here. Significant stories can be repeated many times so that children feel "at home" in them, which gives a shelter and sense of confidence. In Class 1 (age 6–7), the first content for lessons which in later years lead on to history, is classical fairy tales. A sense of inner certainty is created in the child through recurring images, such as that of the youngest of three brothers, who seems to be "simple," but in the end succeeds in finding "the water of life" and becomes the bridegroom of the princess.

The seven–to–eight–year–old in Class 2 readily listens to, paints and acts animal fables and stories of saints, which are archetypal studies of human character and growth. The fox and the hare personify all too human traits. Over against this, a story, such as "St Francis and the Wolf of Gubbio," portrays transformation and ennoblement of the human being. Children of this age have an intuitive perception of human nature, and such images, which become a treasure accompanying them through life, need no explanation.

Eight–to–nine–year–olds in Class 3 take well to the mythological stories of the Old Testament. The tale of the separation of Adam and Eve from their creator and their expulsion from Paradise speak to the child who is gradually becoming more self–aware. Also children who are severely handicapped and/or may suffer the results of childhood deprivation now have an experience of their own identity which calls forth in them a sense for human inter–dependence and human work. Stories from the Old Testament which tell of human beings living and working under the aegis of God and divine law lead on to an introductory study of farming, building and tradesmanship.

The nine–to–ten–year–old in Class 4 easily identifies with the Norse gods and heroes (as previously described). The story of the powerful god Thor, who needs the help of cunning, often malicious, Loki, to retrieve his mighty hammer from the giants, depicts differentiation and interaction of the human character which meet what the child of this age is interested in. The tale of Sigurd the Volsung, an early human hero, who can confront dragons and many enemies single–handed, reflects and strengthens an experience in the child of "I can stand my ground." It provides excellent material for action and drama which can include every child in the class.

The ten–to–eleven–year–old child in Class 5 shows facets in his mental, as well as physical development of the time of ancient Greece, which leads from the mythological age into history. In the course of the year, the stories of gods and demi–gods progress to human biographies. The teacher may choose different characters among her pupils to dramatize and act out some of those mythological or historical individuals. The labours of Herakles and the adventures of the Argonauts are followed by the Trojan War, which is the transition into the beginnings of history. Then the child is ready to imagine and create an understanding for the contrasting lifestyles of Athens and Sparta where the first European culture emerged. The Persian wars and Alexander's conquests, depicting a consolidation of Greek culture and the dawning of individual expression, can appeal strongly to the eleven–year–old.

In the first four classes the history syllabus provided material for the regular story time of the school morning which could then be developed further in plays and practical activities. Now in Class 5 when the "golden heart of childhood" is reached and there is still a balance between play and work (as described previously) the child is ready to begin studying and dwelling on a particular theme for several weeks. Therefore the teacher may now introduce block periods of history. If the class needs it, additional story material can be found in the myths of India, Persia, Babylonia and Egypt.

The eleven–to–twelve–year–old in Class 6 with his awakening intellect can relate to the laws and constitution of Rome. Acting such a character as Julius Caesar can provide an experience of Roman culture. The teacher and her class may try to portray Roman Britain as well as the advent of Christianity. Chosen characteristic scenes from the Middle

Ages, including the life of Charlemagne up to the Crusades, can introduce the child to the age and ideals of knighthood and can give him an
experience of passing from the fortitude of the Roman citizen to the
pious and industrious burgher of the medieval town or burgh. The knight
and the burgher can be complemented by the monk, as exemplified by
St Francis who, with fearless love, could stem the flood of leprosy. The
class can be involved in an experience of the ideals and struggles of
knights, monks and burghers and thereby building stones for later lessons
are laid.

The twelve–to–thirteen–year–old child in Class 7 has the potential to
widen and pursue a great variety of interests. Episodes from the Age of
Discovery and Invention, including the flowering of the Renaissance, are
brought to life in their imagination. Personalities such as Columbus,
Leonardo da Vinci, Wycliffe, Gutenberg and Caxton who laid the foundations of modern civilization can awaken an enquiring mind and en-
thuse the pupils to constructive activity.

To the thirteen– and fourteen–year–old adolescent pupils in Class 8,
a lively survey of history up to the present century is given. The profound influence of the French Revolution and the continuing struggle for
the ideals of freedom, equality and brotherhood, can form an initial
subject. The rise and fall of Napoleon, the wars of independence, and
personalities, such as Benjamin Franklin, can be studied and acted so that
a feeling for the resulting development of modern Europe and America
can be experienced. The pupils may be guided to appreciate how such
inventions as the steam engine and the mechanical loom have changed
our lives.

In this way the young person who turns fifteen in Class 9 can gain
some understanding of the character of the age into which he is born.
The teacher may look again at some aspects of world history, from the
Elizabethan age to modern times and foster an awareness of the driving
motives, ideas and ideals which change civilization with increasing
speed. Acting and studying contrasting personalities such as Mozart and
James Watt, Dickens and Karl Marx, Rutherford and Gandhi or Martin
Luther King provide depth in relating to the modern human spirit. On the
background of history taught in this way a sense for twentieth century
life can develop and may lead to fruitful conversations.

In the last three years of Upper School the teacher supports the young
person in forming at least a feeling and where possible a perception of
history by which he can live and build his own relationship to his time.

This is his birthright regardless of any handicap. Each of these years has a different starting point. The young person who turns sixteen in Class 10 may look once more at the first great cultures of human history. These peoples laid the foundations of our civilization and many of their cultural achievements emerge in a modern way. The class may catch a glimpse of how Greek philosophy laid the basis for education, how agriculture found its beginning in Persia and how the architecture of Egypt experiences a renaissance in our time.

The young person who turns seventeen in Class 11 can be supported in his maturation process in relating to the romances of the Arthurian Knights, Parsifal and the Quest for the Holy Grail. His dignity can be fostered when acting and experiencing such stories as that of Sir Gareth of Orkney who started as a kitchen boy, whose outer battles signify stages of his inner growth; by overcoming the green, red and blue knights, he achieves the clarity and splendour of the white armour. Literature brought to life in this way can build up moral ideals valid for our time. It can help the young person to free his inner humanity and make his own contribution to life.

In Class 12, the final year of school, the young person who turns eighteen can be guided with the help of much visual material and lively action to attempt a survey of history so that a sense of belonging to the development of humankind can grow. The rise, blossoming and decline of different cultures can be vividly imagined. The Greek culture shows all the classical phases of the process. Through such a pursuit the young person can develop a feeling for initiatives from the past and a sense for ideas and ideals of the future. For our pupils in general, it is not important to remember dates and facts of history but no effort should be spared to evoke in them an experience of Man's development from the past to the present and an inner certainty about the worth of the individual who is part of humankind struggling for ideals of the future.


## The chemistry syllabus

In the teaching of sciences an excellent opportunity is given to strengthen the development of the child's enquiring mind independently of his capacity to intellectualize, write down formulas and remember all the details. Pupils are encouraged to take an active part in preparing the experiments, observing and participating in them.

When children become thirteen in Class 7, having been prepared through nature studies such as the physics of heat taught earlier on, chemistry is introduced. They are guided to keep a record in a book by drawing diagrams of experiments and writing short descriptions. Those unable to do this independently are given help or a book is prepared with them. The process of combustion is experienced through experiments involving the burning of dry leaves, wood shavings and other plant matter. The "liberation" of sunlight forces through burning is noted and, according to the ability of the class, discussed. Charcoal–making introduces a variety of by–products and the nature of carbon can be looked at in relation to organic substances. Experiments with sulphur and phosphorus combustion widen the subject to inorganic matter. References can be made to similar processes in the human organism and practical life.

In Class 8 when the young person turns fourteen, he can be introduced to experiments which demonstrate the chemical reactions of sugar, starch, protein and fat to water and fire. These substances have been introduced to him in the nutrition lessons of previous years and their importance for the nourishment of Man can now be further demonstrated. Iodine and Fehling tests and so on can be shown and through these examples an understanding for the vital role of chemical processes in industry can be evoked. In this and the following year industrial visits are arranged whenever possible.

The young person turning fifteen in Class 9 can be introduced to the fermentation of sugar and distillation of alcohol which lead to esters and ether and finally to essential oils. A variety of industrial processes and the social question connected to alcohol can be examined and provide material for lively conversation and humour, drama and other artistic expression. The drilling for oil and its refining form a further chapter this year.

In the last three classes of the Upper School the teaching of chemistry and other sciences is continued in the same visual and practical manner. It is important for our senior pupils to develop the feeling: "I know something about these organic and industrial processes, I have seen them demonstrated." An intellectual understanding is less important for most of them but their capacity should be stretched as far as seems appropriate to the individual. This helps the young adult to integrate into modern life and not feel alienated.

In Class 10 (age 15–16), the polarity of acid and alkali and the formation of salt as the neutral element can be a key subject and can lead on to discovering the phenomena of these organic processes in plant, animal and Man. Opposing forces, such as those of acid and alkali, create harmony in nature. A good example is the bee with the acid juice in its food and the alkali fluid in its blood. The properties and usage of metals can be practically demonstrated and experienced which would lead on to smelting, the formation of alloys and possible visits to related industries.

In Class 11 when young people become seventeen, they can be taken a step further in a selection of experiments which show chemical processes of acids, alkalis and salts. Some chemical elements can become familiar and, in turn, be seen in their wider activity. Sulphur, for instance, is dynamic in the volcanic process of the Earth as well as playing its part in Man's digestive system. By learning to see such substances in their natural activity they can be experienced also as living forces. While our pupils are not usually able to achieve a comprehensive survey of chemistry they may be supported in their last class through many examples to gain a feeling and if possible an understanding for the differences between the processes in Man and the corresponding processes in outer nature. Thereby a sense of healthy balance between Man and outer nature can be fostered.


## English language and the syllabus

Language is a primary tool through which subjects are taught to children from the first to the last school day. We see it as important that the child first listens to the creative, spontaneous language of the teacher and gradually, the natural response of most young children becomes a more conscious formulating of their own creative language. Those children who do not naturally develop speech and need special therapy find great support when they can be helped to participate in the activities of a group whose speech development flourishes. Throughout the years of schooling the pupil should hear and be in the orbit of good, living language, so that an appreciation for language is instilled into him. The true spirit of language can only remain alive through the direct interplay from person to person; in class, between teacher and pupil, and pupil and pupil. The teacher should never tire of being creative in supporting those pupils who cannot speak, to find ways of communicating and understanding others, to gain self-expression and become part of a group.

In the first class we begin with story telling in the form of fairy tales

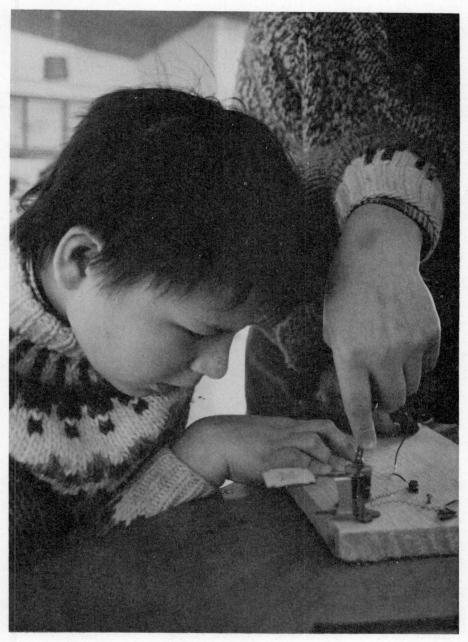

*Learning through experiments in science*

which stimulates the child's imagination. Then the natural world also appears in story form. Here, the challenge to the teacher is, through her warm, clear observation of nature, to create simple stories of the lively interplay between plant and animal, stones, elements and Man. The slender birch tree speaks to the shy rabbit, the tender snowdrop befriends the frozen grass and gives it hope for Spring. The teacher illustrates these stories with her own large and colourful blackboard drawings. She may use glove puppets for children who have difficulty in listening and may lack in word understanding. Out of the story content, simple action games, rhymes and ring games are created, allowing every child in the class to live in the rhythm and beauty of language.

The young child lives in movement and a growing sense of form and these provide the basis for the introduction to reading and writing. By walking, painting and drawing straight and curved lines an inner feeling for their quality is fostered. For some children this can lead to the introduction of writing as an art. For others it is a basic spatial orientation exercise which may have to be worked at for many years. Out of such activity one group can develop an understanding for the meaning of letters: the high mountain, climbed by the prince, takes the form of the "M." As the image "mountain" contains the letter form "M," so the image swan contains the form "S," or the feather the "F." Some may take longer before they reach this stage and actually may achieve but a little writing and then only much later. For others it may be a long road of practising movement and communication skills while reading and writing may be unattainable to them.

As a next step, in Class 2, the teacher may encourage her children to act, illustrate and re-tell, in their own words, animal fables and legends of Saints. Some may then write or copy and illustrate a favourite sentence. In this way, the child's first sentence can be "read." Further sentences may follow and the child's own first reader is thereby created. However, for some children in our classes, it will become a picture book made for them by the teacher. Others, according to ability, can now be guided to recognize their first sentences, learn the individual words and remember the sounds of letters, which they have painted and which have become "old friends."

In Class 3 their souls become more susceptible to expressive sound and movement in the language of poetry, where characteristic sounds help to light up the meaning of words, while rhythms create the mood. Accompanied by lively movement the teacher leads them into the sound, rhythm and imagination of poetry. Some children in our classes can now gradually advance from their personal readers to printed books. At this stage, sentence building, a first element of grammar, can be introduced, as a joyful and humorous activity involving the whole class. Action words, verbs, are closest to the child; when he thinks "to hammer," he wants to hammer with his fists on his desk. Descriptive words, adjectives, leave him more at rest, observing colours and qualities of the world to which he responds with feeling. Whereas the naming word, the noun, is a little more cold and abstract, an object of thinking recognition, separated out from the immediate experience of the child. Games of sentence building address the whole person with his thinking, emotional life and motivation and can involve everyone in the class. Some children may learn to write such sentences with coloured pencils and so distinguish parts of speech. The structure of language the child uses naturally, is quietly raised into consciousness. Thereby the use of language gains a new value which supports the moral development of the child by fostering awareness in his language and social communication.

As the children grow older the teacher's task becomes more diverse: of helping each child actively to participate in some of these class activities and, at the same time meeting the needs of each individual. It requires continuing reassessment and creativity. A child who cannot speak may be a spontaneous actor or may be able to beat the rhythm on a drum while the class speak a poem. A child who has difficulty with writing may be helped to trace over or copy relevant content which has been talked about. In our experience, children who are too withdrawn to take an active part do, nevertheless, benefit from peripheral involvement in group activity. Each pupil needs to be challenged at his own ability level, while simultaneously, his dignity is upheld by participating in class work appropriate for his age.

Let the following examples illustrate these principles. As a class activity, the ten-to-thirteen-year-olds can act the three "fates" of the Northern Myths, spinning and weaving the past, present and future of gods and men, which offers an ideal way to introduce the main tenses. Greek mythology and early history bring many colourful characters full of enterprise and originality who offer material for acting and practising dialogues. A next step can be medieval minstrel tales, followed by stories of travellers and explorers bringing picturesque and dramatic descriptions of what a person has experienced and heard. Most of our pupils who participate in such activities will improve their ability to understand and express themselves. They begin to know of the main tenses, direct and indirect speech, differentiating between one's own and someone else's opinions; reporting what one has lived through or what has been told by another person. Some children can develop this further by writing short essays and simple letters, such as to a local museum to arrange a visit or order materials for the class. Most of our pupils can learn to participate in meaningful conversations which requires coherent language and listening to one another. Some who cannot speak well nevertheless may find other ways of communicating clearly. Others, who do not achieve these skills, continue with special exercises individually or in appropriate groups.

In Class 8 the young adolescent can learn to express himself in a refined manner through familiarity with beautiful language. Lyric poetry evokes expression of his more noble feelings, the epic evolves objectivity and the dramatic portrays the interaction of self and world. These pursuits in the "humanities" provide a balance to his naturally growing interest in the sciences and material world. The whole class can be involved in acting legends such as those of King Arthur and his Round Table giving ideals of virtue and inner strength. This can be followed by presentations of drama which could be scenes from Shakespeare, whose uniquely expressive language can be "soaked in" as living content without the prerequisite of full intellectual understanding. By acting and working with shortened and adapted passages of the Roman and historic dramas adolescents can dive into adult life experience. They can revel in it, play it out in a kind of serious joy, bringing colour and order into the turmoil of their soul. Some pupils who need much support can take silent parts; others may speak just a few words or sentences and a few might learn longer parts or even be able to know the whole class play by heart. Throughout this period individual work, according to ability, must continue. For some it is writing of letters and essays. All the children need encouragement and support to maintain even the smallest steps of progress in their reading and writing or movement and drawing exercises.

In the Upper School, Classes 9 to 12, and beyond that in further education, individual work and literacy continues without interruption. Many of our pupils are unable to read independently. The teacher, therefore, selects readings either to be read to her class or freely told where appropriate, for a short time on a daily basis. Recitation is also practised and conversation fostered. Acting continues to be an essential activity and often culminates in a full dramatic presentation at the end of the

*Drawing of basic forms is an approach to writing*

tenth class after which some of the sixteen–year–old pupils will leave. In our middle and Upper School classes there tends to be an influx of new pupils who could not cope with ordinary secondary school, who may have experienced failure in several schools but who can read and write to some extent and most of whom respond eagerly to the curriculum which we can offer.

For young people from fifteen upwards, the contrast between comedy and tragedy, the lightheartedness and earnestness of life, is the background theme in literature. Shakespeare is again an excellent example where life–stirring events alternate rapidly, or even present themselves side by side, with humour. In prose, Dickens, among others, offers the same subtle and poignant contrast. Guided to make their own discoveries through reciting, listening and comparing without abstract analysis, language as such comes to life for these pupils.

In Class 12, the last year of their schooling, the teacher will try to balance practical training and science lessons with continued practice in poetry and drama, also reading prose with and to her pupils. Reviewing historical developments she can draw upon sources such as the Norse Sagas, Homer's *Iliad*, the romantic poetry of Shelley or Keats which touches the Greek theme. Within these works, archetypal friendship and love are illustrated, which in olden times were restricted to the blood ties of tribe and family. The impulse to free the young individual from such restriction found an historic expression in Shakespeare's *Romeo and Juliet*. This can strike a note in the hearts and minds of young people of our time when they are struggling to become independent people. Pupils who lack the skills of literacy but appreciate the spoken word, can participate in the essence of these studies which help to reach into the depths of their own feelings, to value true friendship and to order and express intimate stirrings such as love and guilt. The class and teacher may choose to study modern writers, poets and dramatists such as Dostoevsky, Christopher Fry, T.S. Eliot, Robert Frost and John Masefield. Most of our pupils are not able to express clearly what these aspects of the Waldorf syllabus have given to them but they can show in their conduct that their social conscience has been stirred. They feel supported as young persons who have to cope with a handicap and are wrestling with their very own individual development.

## *Teaching of number*

The learning of arithmetic and mathematics is closely related to the child's developing ability of co–ordinated movement and spatial orientation. The mental mobility needed for working with mathematics has, as a rule, its roots in physical mobility and harmony of movement, though there are a few exceptions. We can only move a finger or foot in harmony when we have a subtle, subconscious perception of the totality of our movement system, often called the "body image." Likewise, the human being, and more keenly the child, experiences a concept in wholeness, completeness, before becoming aware of the parts or components. The concept "birthday cake" is a primary experience, while knowledge of the ingredients does not build the concept of the whole. In the case of a child who is disturbed and who often comes with an already fragmented picture of the world, we use a method at this stage which can help him to glimpse the "wholeness," a principle which is also basic for the development of morality and social conscience. A child who learns to count by sharing out his sweets to friends develops differently from the child who amasses sweets and counts how many he has gained. Such activities play a part in the formation of thinking habits and lay a foundation which influences the quality of moral thinking in each individual. Therefore, our principle in teaching arithmetic is to start from the whole and subsequently explore the parts.

Accompanied by the teacher's own blackboard drawings, numbers are introduced through stories which convey also qualitative values of numbers such as the wholeness of one and the polarity of two: there is only one sun but day and night are two, two ends and one middle are three, there are four seasons, five petals of the wild rose, and so on. The children are led to counting in sequences, forwards and backwards, through rhythmical movement, running, clapping and jumping. Practical application of counting is exercised in a natural way at moments such as sharing out crayons or cups at breaktime. In fact, in the child's enthusiasm, everything gets counted! Principally, the four rules are introduced simultaneously by the method indicated. Through imaginative stories, games and rhymes, the children discover all kinds of number combinations which are then arranged in all four settings of the four rules. This can lead to the practice of written examples and the construction of number squares. Oral practice of mental arithmetic continues throughout schooling according to ability. The training of memory, at this stage, is important because once the child is ten or older this becomes more difficult without the foundation of early exercising. Therefore, every effort is made to teach number "mobility" (mental arithmetic) including multiplication tables even to pupils who have not yet the intellectual ability to apply them. Simultaneously, the four rules are continued with emphasis on their use in practical life including measurement in length, weight, time and money, leading to the discipline of using standard measurements. For some of our pupils this is not attainable and they continue with movement exercises. For many it is a long way which has to be pursued patiently over many years requiring the tact and persevering enthusiasm of the teacher. She has to lead the children in small steps to discover which of the four rules is needed to solve a practical problem.

Some of our pupils do learn the four rules and can then proceed to long multiplication and division which they should understand before using a calculator. For that group decimals and decimal fractions can be introduced when they are ten or older and with it the understanding of money sums. Few of them are able to learn further complex steps in arithmetic, or make the jump into algebra, as these processes involve logical thinking, which is rarely developed adequately at this stage. Routine practice of all the arithmetic learned is essential and can give great satisfaction.

Geometry, as a new pathway of mathematical activity is introduced in Class 6 and continues throughout the subsequent classes. It is developed from the drawing of forms which have been elaborated since Class 1, with the use of colours and experiencing the beauty of the forms. Now the pupils should learn to draw geometrical figures accurately with ruler and a pair of compasses. Through visual and practical example, basic geometrical laws can become accessible, to a degree, to most pupils. Most will be able to make stars as Christmas decorations and a few will learn to make calculations independently. At the age of twelve, the Theorem of Pythagoras can be introduced visually with colourful constructions, cutting out and building up, leading in degrees to an understanding of the principle. When pupils are fourteen or older they can learn to construct geometrical solids out of clay or cardboard and for some this can link up with the geometrical calculation of area and volume.

In the Upper School we aid pupils to consolidate abilities and skills they have acquired so far and practise their application within society.

*Practising picture–word recognition with an aphasic child*

Pupils often reach a "plateau" or temporary halt but may suddenly blossom in later adolescence and acquire hitherto unexpected skills, especially when motivated through technical application, such as, motor mechanics. Others reach a "plateau" at a later stage and can be guided to use what they know in such practical projects as: the use of money and the telephone, a basic understanding of weights and measures, telling the time, and understanding timetables. Some of our pupils whose intellectual ability is a little retarded, or even average, may be hindered from applying themselves because of their emotional or neurological handicaps. They may make further progress in assimilating concepts and developing abilities, even though at the same time, exhibiting difficulties of memory and/or concentration. Often they can be helped by continued practice of basic abilities already acquired while learning new concepts and solving problems which they perceive as relevant to adult life. To these belong, among others: the management of wages, bills and accounts, the handling of a cheque book and credit card, interest rates and budgeting. Ideally pupils should be allowed to use a calculator only when they have understood the application of the four rules. We prefer that they will do so in the last years of schooling because as much time as possible should be given to the training of their memory and mental agility.

# A year in the life of Class 3

Story material for the whole year can be taken (as described earlier) from the Old Testament, beginning with the Creation and leading up to the Building of the Temple. Man's dialogue with God, our human pathway from Paradise to the Earth, aided by great leaders of ancient times, find an echo in the experience of children who reach the age of nine, independently of their performance or intellectual capacity. All pupils can be involved in such activities as painting the days of Creation, drawing illustrations of the stories with broad wax crayons, building a model of Noah's ark with all the animals. Some pupils may make their first illustrated pre-readers and memorize the days of Creation and the Ten Commandments. Everyone can be involved in acting and listening to stories told with the help of glove puppets. Many children will remember some important events or sequences in a story. Accompanied by these stories, the teacher may give lessons on practical life conducted in block periods: the work of the farmer, through the seasons of the year, can be practised in action rhymes about ploughing, sowing, reaping; the occupations of the miller, the baker, the dairyman, the fisherman and the forester can be explored through songs and practical activity. Every child can be involved with preparing a piece of ground, then with sowing, tending and reaping, with harvesting, grinding the corn and making bread. A visit to a farm can be followed by making butter and cheese in the old way, by hand. A building site is of great interest to children. Together they can build toy houses or a larger play house in the grounds. Some children may learn to identify the main cereals, to name and handle basic tools, to draw houses and a simple ground plan perhaps of the school building.

Based on these activities the teacher can continue with elements of speech, sentence building and grammar as described earlier under "English language and the syllabus" (see page 102).

Eurythmy and gymnastics, music, painting and drawing are part of the life of the class in which everyone participates. Art, with its healing propensities can aid healthy breathing, for instance through painting with water colours. Movement, especially eurythmy as visible speech, can foster word understanding and a love for language. Most children enjoy clapping and walking rhythms, learning the eurythmy movements of some vowels and consonants to poems, and "tone" eurythmy movements to simple melodies and songs (in the scale of C major). Contrasting moods, happy or sad, light and heavy may be performed. Walking or running geometrical forms and exercises with copper rods can further control the body movements and spatial orientation which in turn help the inner movements of thinking. Those children who can imitate movements happily fall in with the eurythmy teacher, others may need individual help. In eurythmy the "ensoulment" of movement is fostered, while gymnastics (introduced as a formal subject in this class) concentrates more on the bodily, physical skills. The latter, including games, supports the growing spatial and social orientation. Energetic exercises with rhythms and verses are used to teach children to skip with a rope and hop, run and jump, start and stop with change of direction and throw and catch a ball. A lesson may be joyfully concluded with social games such as "Cat and Mouse." Here again the class as a whole can be involved and valuable opportunities arise to aid individual children according to their needs.

The joy of singing and making music belong to the daily life of the class. Songs can accompany the seasons of the year and the subjects of the lessons. Simple folk songs with question and answer help the children listen to each other, so does a class orchestra which uses such instruments as recorders, lyres, hand bells, chime bars and percussion. We believe that every child is musical and their individual gifts need to be fostered. One or the other may want individual tuition to learn to play an instrument and may begin to read music and write notes. Playing the recorder fosters the co-ordination between breathing and finger movements. The lyre — a modern stringed instrument designed for our work — brings harmony to the whole child and almost everyone can learn to play a percussion instrument. Music-making is a social activity which brings joy to everyone.

In art lessons the class should become quiet to experience the moods of colours: the radiating of yellow, the enclosing of blue and the prominence of bright red. The children paint with water colours using broad brushes on wet paper. After experiencing those primary colours they discover imaginative forms which arise out of their meeting and interplay. Many of our children need guidance to make flowing brush strokes, to rinse the brush and keep the paints clean; as they acquire the basic skill they are encouraged to compose pictures freely. While painting requires separate lesson time, drawing is a daily activity. Each child has a large "main lesson" book in which the teacher's blackboard illustrations and some words or sentences can be copied using initially broad wax crayons. All children are encouraged to take a pride in their own book. Some can begin to compose their own drawings and text, others need much individual help and for some the pictures have to be drawn with them by the teacher. In this way every child in the class can be involved. Time is also set aside for free-drawing and drawing exercises. Children are taught shading, where form arises out of light and heavy, short and long strokes of the crayon. Some may need extra practice in drawing the human form with head, trunk and limbs.

A special therapeutic subject which can now be introduced is form drawing. Children may learn to walk and run simple, then increasingly complicated, patterns drawn on the floor and afterwards draw these in special books. They may begin with pre-writing patterns, proceed to form completion exercises and eventually copy or even design Celtic border patterns. Emphasis is laid upon clear distinction between straight and curved lines and increasing accuracy. These lessons, which require so much discipline and concentration, can in turn give great satisfaction

*"This is my favourite story!"*

to individual children as they can be finely graded to their needs. They may continue throughout their years of schooling.

The arts should always be complemented by crafts. In addition to the use of tools, the children of this class have handwork lessons. These offer the possibility of training the child's thinking capacity, enjoying beauty through developing skills, and increasing his hand–eye coordination (threading a needle!). Each child can be guided according to his need and ability: finger crocheting, simple weaving with double knitting wool, lead up to knitting and crocheting. A handwork teacher may help children in the relaxed atmosphere of such a lesson to talk about some of their most personal thoughts and feelings while those who cannot yet express themselves in words can participate in this mood and all children, some with much help, can enjoy beautiful and practical articles produced. Some may make knotted puppets and then perform little stories for themselves and others.

It becomes increasingly apparent in this year that the teaching of reading, writing and number work has to be finely graded according to individual need and ability. However, an appreciation of language and number is important for all children. Some who have more severe handicaps attend separate special groups and classes which offer movement exercises, basic spatial and body orientation, recognition of objects and so on. The others have daily lessons in which pre–reading, writing and number activities are practised and those whose intellectual ability is average work with readers and arithmetic books, write to dictation, practise spelling and free composition. As in all subjects, also here, the teacher will use an artistic approach and not neglect accuracy and intellectual learning. She may use the subjects currently taught in main lesson to help the children make their own readers and number work books with illustrations while also using published modern reading and number work schemes as suitable. Our pupils' ability levels may vary greatly with regard to different skills. A child may learn to read but may be unable to write, may be able to count by rote but be unable to apply number to practical situations and vice versa. Much skill and ingenuity is required of the teacher to assess each child's ability and needs correctly, to help them at this age to lay the best foundation for their further learning.

# A year in the life of Class 6

In Class 6 when the children become twelve and are approaching adolescence, their varying abilities become more apparent and the teacher
will take particular care that her pupils support each other and continue
together as a group. There may be an influx of new children, some
who feel they have failed at previous schools, some who feel rejected
by their parents. Here they can become "stars" in the class and learn
to support their less able peers who in turn may give encouraging love
and joy. Geography and history and the new subjects for this class,
physics, geology and astronomy, taught in block periods give plenty of
opportunity for such interaction. They will be taught in the same method
as described above, for Class 3: lessons will be introduced with lively
movement and musical activity, reciting and listening to poems, followed by a brief presentation of the main subject out of which further
practical, artistic and therapeutic activity is developed. We have already
referred to the contents of the history, geography and chemistry syllabus and now add a description of the new subjects for this class. In
physics, acoustics, optics, heat, magnetism and electricity are introduced for about two weeks each. Pupils are, in a practical way, involved in experiments and are taught to observe and listen. The
experiments are placed into the context of life, everyday situations and
nature. With most pupils the teacher can draw on experiences in music,
painting and movement in previous years. Some pupils may prefer to
be peripheral observers, most become eagerly involved in practical
experimentation and some may achieve a first understanding of physical
laws.

An introduction to geology arising out of previous geography lessons
offers another opportunity for the growing child to awaken his interest
for the ground under his feet. Field trips to a quarry, a limestone cave,
a rocky mountain, depending upon the nearby geological structure, can
present good material for observation, drawing, conversation, and also,
for some, making simple geological maps.

The down–to–earth "study" of geology can well be balanced and
widened by an introduction to astronomy. Most pupils can learn to
observe the sun's path through the course of the year and the waxing and
waning phases of the moon. Artistic and colourful geometric drawings
of the events in the sky can be produced and home–made star charts may

adorn the classroom. Age–old legends about the star constellations offer good story material for this age group.

Further opportunities to become involved with life in a practical way are presented to these adolescents in handwork, woodwork and gardening. These can give them a feeling of harmony and satisfaction. They learn to make such toys and articles as dolls, animals, simple slippers and cushions. They may be helped or encouraged to work independently in designing, cutting and sewing material and when appropriate, embroidering the finished article. The first steps in woodwork are learning to use saw, rasp, gouge, chisel and mallet. Sawing a piece of wood and rasping it into a darning egg can form a first exercise. Each child should then make, or be helped to make a mallet for his own use. Articles such as wooden spoons, bowls or bird–houses can be cut, chiselled and rasped, sanded and oiled. The pupils should have an experience of making an object, both useful and pleasing to look at, even though, in some cases, the teacher has had to make it with them and, in the case of a very few children, for them. Gardening is another subject which can involve all pupils of the class as even those who are physically disabled can gain from observing and being part of the group. Preparing the soil, sowing and planting, regular tending and finally harvesting, are important experiences for all while planning the work and identifying plants can be learned according to ability.

Art work permeates all the lessons and also requires separate sessions. The drawing of diagrams in physics lessons is a new skill to be practised in main lesson but in separate sessions, projection can be introduced by drawing objects lit up on one side, including their shadows. At this stage it should be done free hand and also those children who need much help may gain an experience of the interplay between light and shadow. In painting the awareness of depth and distance can be fostered through exercises in colour perspective and the introduction of a new technique which is painting on dry paper with several washes of water colour, allowing the paint to dry after each wash. In singing and making music the qualities of major and minor keys can be particularly enjoyed by children of this age as well as part songs and more demanding rounds. Participating in a class orchestra supports the social development, and instrumental playing can give personal satisfaction to individual pupils. In eurythmy, emphasis can now be laid on vigorous and definite movements such as copper rod exercises, precise walking of geometric forms, and the movements of sounds to poems with strong alliteration. As a balance to this, the pupils can then respond with a certain depth of feeling when they are introduced to the "tone" eurythmy movements for musical intervals and the contrasting moods of major and minor. In gymnastics they enjoy rhythmical movement exercises requiring precise body control. An introduction to the Greek pentathlon of running, jumping, wrestling, disc and javelin throwing with emphasis on style, rhythm and accuracy rather than speed and strength can now open up a new field of experience and healthy exercising. All the musical, artistic and gymnastic lessons allow the teacher to place before each child well graded challenges while involving the whole class as a group.

In the teaching of English and number, care and skill is required of the teacher to meet the increasingly diverse needs and ability levels of her pupils and simultaneously foster the social interaction and maturation of her class as a whole. As a daily exercise ordered conversation can be practised even including non–speaking children in the group, helping each one to become more aware of how they express themselves and communicate. Listening to and speaking poetry continues, as does the practice of improvised and formal acting. Regular reading aloud by the teacher to the class of brief passages of classical literature from the medieval times offers to the whole class content which can become treasures in their minds and souls for life. Those who have little word understanding are helped by listening, for short regular periods, to well written language, and to those who can read guidance for further reading is given. The teacher will, in addition, use available schemes for the practice of reading, writing, and spelling. Some pupils who are at a pre-reading stage or have no access to the spoken word, require separate sessions with appropriate special exercises. The same holds good for the practice of numeracy. However, aspects of formal geometry can be introduced to the whole class, the first geometrical laws can be discovered together, by drawing large scale on the floor, or on the blackboard with large compasses and string. The practice of numbers and geometrical forms can involve the whole class in much movement and practical activity, however, emphasis will now be laid on individual work.

# Classes 11, 12 and beyond

A number of our pupils will leave at the age of sixteen after completing the tenth class. Some want to go home, others wish to become more independent and can move into their own accommodation with support, if needed. Others who need very specialized, perhaps physical care, may find a placement for young adults where this can be provided. We make every attempt to support our school leavers to find the best place in accordance with their wishes and needs. Those who continue with us for further schooling, education and training have decided to do so in consultation with parents, ourselves and sending authorities. Of these some can benefit from continued schooling and others, who have more severe handicaps, will follow a course of social and practical training.

Our Further Schooling Programme continues to make use of the Waldorf syllabus. The "senior pupils" of the Class 11 (age 16–17), have a daily "main lesson" for the first hour every morning and geography, history, chemistry, botany, physics and technology are presented according to the same method as described above but with increased emphasis on their practical application. It makes a great difference to young people to have participated in taking apart and putting together again a telephone, a radio, a motor and other machines and gadgets used in everyday life. Some will achieve a practical and limited theoretical understanding while others may at least have an improved sense for how such machines should be treated. This supports them in finding their way in life.

In the winter and early spring terms the senior pupils spend the rest of the morning expanding their "life and communication skills," doing art work, practising English and number work. In the afternoons small groups go, through a rotation of block periods of learning crafts in our workshops, such as rug–weaving, metalwork, woodwork, basket-weaving, pottery, toy–making and candle–making. Craft work improves their manual skills, conveys an experience of handling natural materials and provides the satisfaction of producing useful articles. They have a full day which concludes with an evening programme of sports, drama, and a weekly "house evening" when past experiences can be mutually assessed and future plans are made. Social games and dancing also play an important role. In the summer and autumn terms workshop activities take place in the morning. Afternoons are spent working on group projects planned and designed together and practically seen through to completion. These may include constructing a playground for younger children, building a path, a retaining wall, putting up a fence. At times senior pupils may also learn to help on the farm.

Our Class 12 pupils, aged 17 to 18, have school on a day release basis and those who are sufficiently independent may have work experience placements with local tradesmen in town. Canteens, old people's homes and others may give them opportunities. They may have three or four such placements in the course of a year. Those who are not independent enough to go out may have work placements within the wider circumference of our own organization to achieve as much independence as is possible for the individual. Some who find that they cannot yet cope with their placement in town can alternatively spend a time gaining more work experience in our own setting and then try to go out again. Our senior pupils form a strong peer group and value the experience of mutual assessment and shared counselling sessions. Experience has shown that most of them would wish and could benefit from expanding the senior school programme for another year. As a future development we therefore plan to initiate a flexible programme which would offer them a place in a Class 12 structured in a similar way to Class 11 and then a Class 13 with individual work placements and day release schooling.

# 6 The assessment process

## The meaning of assessment in Camphill

Regular assessment constitutes an essential part of our work. Our philosophy implies that Curative Education is a reciprocal process between educator and pupil, so each assessment of a pupil and his situation requires an equal emphasis on the self–examination of the educator. From this it follows that assessment is not limited to a pupil's scholastic progress, social integration and personality development, but necessitates also a continued re–evaluation of our diagnostic insights and therapeutic attitudes. The purpose of our continuing assessment procedures is to deepen further our understanding of the individual pupil and to inspire and give direction to our therapeutic intervention. Pupils come to us because the course of their lives call for such intervention: to meet this call requires the healing will, individually and communally, of all those who work here in whatever capacity or profession.

## Medical assessment

The process of assessment begins on receipt by the Schools of an initial enquiry regarding a placement, the perusal of the accompanying documentation and the decision to offer an interview based on the information provided. Great care is taken at this stage because the admission to Camphill means an important intervention in a child or young person's life. Careful consideration must be given to his own and his family's individual needs including his different levels of maturing in relation to his age and our possibilities of providing a healing environment and education.

The initial interview marks an important first meeting of the child and his family with Camphill, represented in this instance by the Schools' medical officer. If it is conducted at the Schools it also offers an opportunity for the prospective pupil, his parents and others concerned, to look around the Schools and meet our staff. A searching developmental and social history is elicited from the parents, based primarily on the mother's experience of her child, to which great importance is attached. She (and usually, to a lesser extent, the father) is the person who really *knows* the child, not only through observation but mainly through her very personal inner connection and shared living experience. The history related by the mother is of a different value than the more scientifically based information which is obtained from the reports provided by teacher, psychologist, social worker, and other professionals who have worked with, tested or treated the child (and his family). The evaluation includes time spent with the child and a brief physical examination. Apart from the greeting and farewell, the parents and the child are seen separately and, equally, any professional accompanying the child or family is given a space of privacy.

All these elements of the consultation are necessary in order to achieve a full and balanced assessment of the child. All children now referred to the Schools are "recorded" by the sending local authority which has included a medical examination and vision and hearing testing. For the staff of the Camphill Schools a broad picture of the child and his needs is important in deciding on the admission and the suitability of placement in a particular house, group and class. If the child is subsequently admitted the contact established at these interviews forms an important basis of ongoing relationship and trust between parents and school doctor. Where the application does not lead to an admission, advice on alternative placements, management questions and future re-referral, where appropriate, naturally follows. It is helpful for a child who has special needs if parents and professionals recognize soon enough the time for appropriate intervention in his school career. Young children are open and receptive to change and we can often help them in a more profound way than is possible if they are older on admission; with adolescence their organism and their ways tend to set into definite patterns. It is in many ways more difficult, often too late, if action is taken only after a young person's situation at home and/or in school, has broken down. There may also be a history of failures. Nevertheless, we do also admit adolescents and young adults — but then we can do so much less for them and it is an uphill struggle.

Once the child or young person commences at Camphill and has settled into life in his class and family unit, he is again seen by one of the Schools' doctors whose recorded observations serve as a baseline for monitoring personality growth and development, sensory functioning and the child's general physical wellbeing. At a later stage, these observations may be supplemented by consultations with other specialists.

# Assessment within home and school life

## Informal assessment

The staff members of the family unit in which the child is living discuss particular problem areas as they arise. These may include questions of communication and guidance, stimulating independence and self-reliance, also problems of behaviour and discipline which may test the attitudes and resourcefulness of the adult community in the house. The teacher may discuss specific learning disabilities, social integration or any other problems arising in class with other members of the Teachers' College. Difficulties in the home unit are frequently reflected in behaviour in the classroom or the other way round, so regular communication between teacher, houseparent, group-parent and, where relevant, therapist is fostered. Houseparents can take a pupil to see our resident doctors, in their surgery, who may prescribe medical treatment. On the doctor's advice further consultations with specialists in the hospital services or with our own therapists or senior staff may be arranged.

## Formal Assessment

The group-parent, under the guidance of her houseparents, is required to keep a diary on pupils in her care and enter regular reports in our case-records. Annually, a full report on each pupil is written and sent to the parents and the sending local authority. These reports attempt to present a picture of the pupil's trials and triumphs and comprise the following:

a. An extensive teacher's report on maturity traits, the pupil's response to each subject taught, progress in 3 R's and in other lessons such as gym, eurythmy, music, handwork, crafts.

b. A descriptive and in–depth report by the houseparent on the development of the child throughout the past year. Areas covered include maturation, social integration and/or behaviour problems, communication, independence and acquired skills.

c. A report by therapists on special therapeutic measures.

d. A report by a nurse on the physical health, including weight and height and any medical treatment received.

The "clinic" in Camphill is an important and integral activity in the care, education and guidance of our pupils and has a different emphasis from the more conventional case conference. Our clinics have a twofold task: firstly, we attempt to gain an image of the whole, undamaged personality "behind" whatever handicap the pupil suffers. ("Handicap" is generally seen in the context of child development and can often be understood as an exaggeration or one–sidedness of facets of human development leading to a specific pathology.) Secondly, we try to form a picture of the pupil's strengths and weaknesses, progress and problem areas which helps us to decide on remedial measures, therapies and medication.

To achieve this objective our medical staff work together with the pupil's teacher, houseparents, group–parent and, when applicable, special therapist and any other member of staff whose advice they want to call on. Each participant reports on the work done, progress made and problems encountered and examples of school and craft work are made available. The pupil then joins the clinic, is asked about school and home life, and if able, given the opportunity to express his views on relevant issues and future concerns. He might also be invited to demonstrate certain basic skills. Subsequently, when he has left the room, an attempt is made to form a comprehensive picture of the pupil's present situation. A pupil who is mentally impaired and suffers from epilepsy, for example, might also have behaviour problems and specific learning difficulties. These problems may cause communication and contact disorders, which can be helped better if we understand whether he is over–sensitive to his environment, or perhaps lacking in awareness of other peoples' needs and feelings. These factors are relevant in trying to assess aspects of the child's physical and psychological development and Ego integration. By the latter we mean the way in which his spiritual, undamaged individuality relates at present to his own body, his emotional life and his environment, including other people. Only then can we determine remedial exercises, define therapeutic approaches and the doctor can prescribe therapies and/or medication. Clinics are held annually for each pupil but can be repeated more often when needed, for example, if his parents wish to attend. Both the clinics and the College Meetings, described below, are important learning situations for the students in the Curative Education Course who are involved in the education and care of the pupils.

We use the term "College Meeting" to describe a multi–disciplinary gathering, a convocation which focuses exclusively on one particular pupil. The College Meeting is at the heart of Camphill's therapeutic work and endeavour, aiming truly to understand the child or young person in depth and thereby improve our own attitudes and the web of social intercourse with and around him. Ideally we should be able to change our own ways so that a warm and healing will can help the growing child or developing young person to cope in the best possible way with his own handicap and difficulties and learn together with others to make his contribution to life. Therefore, a College Meeting makes special demands on the inner preparedness of each staff member and student to learn, to change and to develop that healing will. The meeting is held in the evening after the children have been settled so that there is peace in the house and all those who know the child can participate: the entire staff of the pupil's family unit and doctors, teachers, therapists and any others who can be helpful. Usually the evening is guided by a doctor or senior staff member, but the true leader and teacher of the evening is the chosen child himself, although outwardly not present. This meeting, which begins and ends with a prayer, is underpinned by our active faith that it will change something in the experience of the participants which in turn affects the child's own being and future development. We believe that this holds good even when, later on, there are further difficulties.

The College Meeting has three distinct parts in which interest, compassion and conscience are the directing stars. The first part is a presentation of the child's history, personal, social and medical, including the early milestones and the child's development up to the time of his admission. Contributions are thoroughly prepared and are presented with a sense of deep respect and tact towards the child and his family, without judgment but with clarity and human warmth. Then the houseparents, teachers, and where appropriate, therapists as well as others concerned, will describe the child's development and present situation here with us. Samples of his school, art and craft work may be presented. Great care is taken to look at his physical constitution. By the time this part has been completed a vivid image of the child has arisen, built up through clear observation and painted on the "canvas" of human warmth.

The second part of the meeting is opened by three guiding questions: "What does it feel like to be this child or young person?" "How does he experience himself and his environment of which we are a part?" and: "What might be his personal aims in this life?" True entering into these questions requires the effort of leaving self behind and going out into the situation of another. In as much as we can achieve it, each one will gain new perspectives which can lead to profound changes of our views and even in the conduct of our personal lives. Thereby, we may create the social conditions which are a fertile "soil" for a better, and hopefully new understanding. The attempt to gain a clear diagnostic picture of the pathology which the child has to cope with is an aspect of the College Meeting but it also aims at something more than this. It is a living process of awareness and human growth which leads from true empathy into an active and unsentimental compassion. The third part is opened with the question: "What can we do?" The answers come from our conscience, should fire our motivation and provide ample space for therapeutic ingenuity. They have to be practical and usually mean that decisions about new attitudes and therapeutic measures will have to be upheld and carried through faithfully for a considerable span of time. Each meeting is unique because each individual is unique. Nevertheless, the following summary of a typical College Meeting may serve as a picture of our endeavour (some fifteen staff and students were involved in the meeting which lasted over two hours).

John was rejected at birth by his natural mother and taken "into care" by a local social work department. At an early stage he was placed with a not inexperienced foster mother. She herself was a somewhat anxious person but held on to him against considerable opposition from her husband. The child was intellectually only slightly retarded but hyperactive and difficult. He was expelled from the local primary school but was too intelligent and also too disruptive for the local ESN school. Eventually the foster mother came near to breakdown and her own family threatened to disintegrate. Therefore, the local psychological services, supported by the social work department, applied to our Schools to provide residential education for John. He was admitted here at the age of eight. One of our first tasks was to gain the confidence and support of the foster mother and her social worker, both of whom, in their own way, felt that they had failed. Once these were tentatively achieved John stopped absconding and began to settle down here. He was a bright, outgoing and active child with a rather large head, dark hair and shining brown eyes. He had a good complexion but his breathing was shallow. He was quick and often witty in conversation but his relationships to his peers seemed to be as shallow as his breathing. He seemed to relate quickly to our staff who felt that the boy had something appealing and felt drawn to love him. However, he did test out the attitude and reaction of every staff member by being destructive, cruel to other children, pilfering and absconding. When his undesirable behaviour was met with consequential measures taken by his group parent, houseparents or teacher, John seemed to feel rejected which in turn enhanced his problems. His hyperactivity added to the difficulty as it prevented him from concentrating for any length of time. Consequently, he could not make full use of his natural intelligence nor pay sufficient attention to whatever he was doing, so he appeared to be clumsy. The first real breakthrough was achieved by the teacher in the classroom. John absorbed the curriculum presented in his class and especially the artistic approach, as a dry sponge absorbs water. Soon he made sure not to miss his lessons but he still occasionally absconded in the middle of the night.

In the College Meeting we became aware that John's experience of himself was that of a fairy–tale king — large–headed with a crown: everything his eyes saw was his possession and other people were his subjects. The fact that the world did not comply with this self–experience and had rejected him caused an endless chain of frustration which drove him into a spiral of self–destruction. His large head, short neck and shallow breathing presented a telling picture of his difficulty in establishing a healthy relationship between self and world. He had not established a social "breathing" process, was too possessive of "his" adults and tended to reject his peers. Equally he was driven to appropriate anything shining and, in his eyes, attractive. His hands had to take it and, consequently, he could not establish an adequate concept of "something belonging to other people," a condition which caused a degree of "moral blindness."

We decided to avoid any direct requests, but rather convey an attitude which takes it as a matter of course that a king will reach his greatest fulfilment in serving the needs of his subjects. Special stories, centring around this theme, were told to him. He was to be guided to perform small daily household duties to serve the needs of others. Most important were all those artistic activities which would deepen his breathing, both physiologically and in social intercourse. He was to be given repeated periods of painting therapy, curative eurythmy and, as he grew older, riding therapy. His group-mother, with the support of senior staff, was encouraged always to "be a step ahead" of him. She should try to prepare him for any unforeseen situations and changes in routine and develop a perception for his emotional reactions. She should help him use his lively imagination for creative social pursuits and artistic activity so that these would gradually replace his destructive and self-destructive tendencies. We could foresee that there would be lapses but felt confident that the boy had a good chance to mature. Also, great care would have to be taken to improve our relationship to his foster mother and social worker. He would need their regular visits here and would have to be certain that he could go home for holidays.

In retrospect it can be said that he responded well, but also that there were lapses such as absconding and on one occasion, for a brief while, successfully pretending to the police that he was a deaf and dumb boy from a faraway town, stranded here. His group-mother developed a sense of deep gratitude to John because he helped her self-education as no-one else had done.


*Reviews* and *case conferences* are held when requested by parents, sending authorities and/or ourselves usually taking place at our Schools or local authority premises. We welcome opportunities of sharing concerns with parents and professionals, indeed are always prepared to provide hospitality or travel to meetings in other locations. The mutual understanding and the sharing of progress and problems are vital to the wellbeing of the pupil and his family. Particularly important are Future Needs Assessments required by law when pupils have reached adolescence and school leaving comes into sight (although many prefer to stay on until they are young adults). In exceptional circumstances, such as when our pupils' safety seems to be at risk or when a senior pupil wants to leave school earlier than had been planned together with him, then he or we may call for an emergency case conference.

# 7 Medical and therapeutic care

## Medical care

The medical care of pupils, staff and their dependants is provided by the Camphill Medical Practice. This is a restricted National Health Service (NHS) practice run by three doctors, two of whom live in the community. The practice also offers medical care to the other Camphill Communities in the area. The doctors work together with two visiting consultants, a psychiatrist and a psychologist, and six to eight residential nurses, a midwife and a group of therapists who provide physiotherapy, speech, music and riding therapy, curative eurythmy, painting and play therapy and counselling. There is a close liaison with medical specialists, psychologists and social workers, both locally and in the pupils' home areas. In keeping with the ethos of our community life all the resident specialists also take their share in other responsibilities, supporting houseparents and teachers.

With the high level of staffing and the facilities available, we can supervise regular drug treatment and provide the care required for conditions such as epilepsy and severe psychosis. Similarly, for most acute illnesses, as well as for the rare instances of terminal illness, we can often offer the necessary care in one of our sick bays. It is possible for most of the staff children to be born at home, attended by a qualified midwife. We see these as important experiences in community life. It is a natural extension of our curative educational and therapeutic endeavours to allow such fundamental human events and efforts to colour and enrich it.

Illness and handicap are not necessarily perceived as unfortunate accidents of nature to be avoided, suppressed or stopped in their tracks at all costs; we view them as part of human existence which, besides

131

being debilitating at times, can equally be strengthening and a source of learning and self–knowledge, if we are open to it. It is known that human beings (and all living organisms) have inherent self–regulating and healing forces. Medical and therapeutic care can then be seen as supporting and promoting healing as well as developmental and maturational processes. In certain circumstances, we make use of pain killers, antibiotics (literally "against life"), anticonvulsants and various other "antidrugs" which are available, but these rarely, if ever, promote healing; generally their action is to contest symptoms. This is not a blanket condemnation of conventional medicine, for the role of surgery and replacement therapy (insulin, thyroxin, and so on) is irrefutable in appropriate and limited circumstances.

As a broad approach, therapeutic measures complementary to medical treatment have much to offer as first line treatment in many acute self-limiting illnesses, but equally in chronic conditions and developmental handicaps. A starting point is the diet, which is basically wholefood, much of it organically produced in our own vegetable gardens and small-holding. Junk–foods, drinks and food additives are kept to a minimum and a balanced diet is encouraged. Where appropriate, special diets are used. Secondly, therapies such as physiotherapy, massage, body oiling and so–called oil–dispersion baths with natural plant oils, and various artistic therapies (as described later in this chapter) are prescribed for various illnesses and handicaps. The medical treatment used is based primarily on anthroposophical, homeopathic and herbal remedies which are prescribed for their activity in promoting the healing forces, referred to earlier. Where necessary, these treatments are supplemented with conventional allopathic medicines. The latter are used as infrequently as possible, for as short a duration and in as low a dosage as is therapeutically appropriate, due to their frequent side–effects. All these treatments are provided within the scope of the NHS practice.


# Therapies and therapeutic exercises

Therapies are prescribed by a doctor in clinical consultations or at College Meetings but can be based on observations and suggestions made by any member of staff. At that stage, doctors, houseparents, teachers and therapists can be equally involved. The prescriptions are then taken up by the Therapy College which has to consider the best sequence and timing of a variety of therapies having regard of the individual needs of pupils and the availability of therapists. The College also keeps a record of therapies prescribed, taking place or waiting to be taken up. Further, the therapists and their students, working in groups appropriate to their different disciplines, have to work out details of applying a therapy, conduct studies and research, and provide mutual consultation and support. The therapies and progress of pupils are then reviewed in the following clinics as well as in the College and groups concerned.

The whole life of our community has therapeutic aims and the overall curriculum based on the family units and the classroom syllabus, provide a "healing" education. Many children and young people need additional help to make the best use of the education offered here and to achieve a greater fulfilment of their potential in maturation and independence. Often such help can be provided by individually designed special therapies which take up the threads of a child's development where it has been stunted, delayed or broken off.

As an example we can think of a ten–year–old who had reached the word understanding of a child of two years but his expressive speech had not advanced beyond the eighteen month level. This situation caused him great frustration which expressed itself in hyperactivity and aggression. A special sequence of riding therapy, movement and speech therapy and curative eurythmy then provided an essential help for him. As his speech progresses, his frustration recedes, he can make better use of the school syllabus and improve his social integration.

The difference between education in general and a particular therapy, as used here, can be compared with the difference of providing a good diet and giving a medicine. While therapies are prescribed to improve the wholeness of a human being they always aim to aid specific aspects within the living organism, the emotional development and the Ego integration. They should help these three to interweave and come to expression in the social maturation of the person. A therapy which therefore, wants to reach a particular organic, emotional or mental process, usually uses only one specific medium at the time, such as movement, colour, music or the spoken word. Careful consideration is given to the choice and the particular way in which it is applied, also having regard to the age and sensitivity of the individual. Therefore, a combination of scientific knowledge, artistic creativity and the related skills in art and crafts is needed. Further, each therapy has its own rhythm, daily, three times or once a week; for a term, six months or six weeks at a time with a break of six weeks in between. These therapies usually require a strictly individual application but some can be suitably conducted in groups. Obviously special rooms providing an adequate environment are needed as well.

We will describe a selection of special therapies. In broad terms, four approaches can be seen and, even though there is no strict division between them, we shall try to characterize them:

a. Physical therapies such as physiotherapy, patterning, massage, oiling, special baths, hydrotherapy, trampolining and therapeutic gymnastics.

b. Therapies which work more directly on the living organic processes of the body such as curative eurythmy, music therapy, coloured light therapy.

c. Therapies which can work directly on the sensory and emotional experience and have a secondary but well–aimed effect on the health and harmony of a child such as curative eurythmy and music therapy (for the latter two this refers to other aspects than those considered under b), listening space therapy, coloured shadow therapy, painting therapy and other therapies which enhance the experience of touch, smell, taste, balance and warmth, also riding therapy.

d. Therapies which help the Ego integration (our understanding of this process is characterized further in Chapter 8). They may be play therapy, drama therapy and individual counselling. Speech therapy and aphasic treatment, amongst others, may make use of all the above mentioned elements.

## Physiotherapy

To help children who have movement impairments several different therapies are available at our Schools. Those with cerebral palsy can have conventional physiotherapy and this need not be described here. As a follow–up and for certain children who have movement problems, for instance, in connection with aphasia, *patterning* exercises are applied. This is a therapy based on the idea that a child's embryonic and early motor development, in certain respects, is a recapitulation of the evolution of the movement patterns shared with the animal kingdom and leading to human movements. It is essential to diagnose correctly at which phase of life a child's movement development halted so that the further phases can be practised by moving the child's limbs and head passively until the movement patterns are "imprinted" into the child's own system. The development begins with homolateral patterns and progresses to crosslateral patterns, crawling and finally walking. The healthy achievement of crosslateral walking is seen as a step in the development of laterality (dominance of one cerebral hemisphere), and hence to speech and language. We practise patterning exercises usually for no longer than five to fifteen minutes, twice a day. They are carefully supervised by a therapist or doctor but can be executed by other members of staff. This treatment can be supplemented or followed up by massage, curative eurythmy, trampoline and/or therapeutic gymnastic exercises.

The trampoline can be used both as a diagnostic aid to show up motor disabilities, and as a therapeutic tool to overcome such disabilities. The liberating effect of being free of gravity for brief moments can be healing in itself. The co-ordination and balance required for jumping is a useful discipline which can be developed into various therapeutic exercises appropriate for different handicaps. As a rule children begin on the trampoline with homolateral crawling (right arm moves forward with right leg, and so on) and then practise crosslateral movements which are both eased and emphasised by the resilience of the trampoline's elastic surface. The next stages are bouncing on hands and knees, often surprisingly difficult to control, and jumping in the upright position; this may need much encouragement and guidance for children and young people who have more severe motor handicaps. Thereafter, specific jumping rhythms can be helpful, for example children who have epilepsy are guided gradually to increase the height of jumping to a certain maximum and then decrease it. Those who have poor gross motor control, for instance when they suffer from a degree of athetosis, benefit from learning to jump in a regular rhythm and height, and also by coming to a sudden halt with bent knees. Various rhythms of jumping, and more complicated exercises, can be used to enhance co-ordination and balance generally and for specific conditions. The improvements in a child's uprightness and general co-ordination can help him towards clearer speech and healthy thinking.

## Bothmer gymnastics

For the child who has special needs, Bothmer gymnastics is a valuable aid in enhancing his general physical and mental awareness. Developed in 1922 by Graf Fritz von Bothmer under the auspices of Rudolf Steiner and the Waldorf School movement, Bothmer gymnastics has been in increasing demand for its educational element and healing qualities. In Camphill, it can be part of a weekly gymnastics lesson. The exercises are built up for each class according to the progressing age and maturity of the pupils aged nine to eighteen years. For children entering puberty, for example, and who begin to feel themselves and their limbs as though weighed down to earth, there is an exercise called "Fall into Space." It allows the child the experience of overcoming the heaviness he feels, which gives him a sense of his own uprightness. Disciplined rhythmical exercises form the beginning and end of each lesson. For the child who has a handicap, accomplishing a physical exercise is a tremendous boost to self–confidence and learning capabilities. What is experienced as controlled, directed movement is later translated into energy for thinking. Bothmer gymnastics enhances physical ability, spatial integration, gives a sense of worth and dignity. As a therapy, it can help with many different impediments: for the child needing positive correction with regard to his social behaviour or with too little motivation, or perhaps too little self–awareness; and the child who is lacking in concentration and is easily distracted, as well as for children with orientation and spatial disturbances. Therapeutic Bothmer gymnastics can be given in group sessions to three or four children or to single children two to three times during the week for a period of some weeks; during this time the children are allowed to enter a therapeutic space specially created for them and within that space they are given a series of exercises which are repeated for as long as necessary. Repetition of the exercises, with gradual increasing mastery, is very important, for through that a harmonizing of the disturbance can take place.

Steven came regularly to Bothmer gymnastics therapy for about nine months. He was a tall, slim, hyperactive boy with orientation, co–ordination, speech and learning difficulties. He was as restless as a butterfly, here, there and everywhere, but never for long. The aims were to improve concentration, to achieve greater sensitivity of fine motor co-ordination, to create distance between himself and his surroundings (orientation), all leading to an enhanced thinking ability, to help him learn to think with the aid of his limbs. He enjoyed coming because he was given a space and time specially created for him, with his particular needs in mind which included undivided attention from the therapist. There was room for play and for some hard, disciplined work. As he was hyperactive, Steven's powers of concentration were not great at first, but gradually, as he began to detect an improvement in his abilities, his concentration improved too. He is musical and this was his saving grace enabling us to work on rhythm and fine motor control through movement and his musicality. Although slowly at first he learned to distinguish between long and short, loud and soft, large and small, fast and slow; then randomly and quickly, at a moment's notice. This required presence of mind, co-ordination and agility. To balance the light side of our therapeutic session we also did some slow, measured exercises so that Steven might finish the session in a peaceful and relaxed way. Very important for him was the interaction between himself and the therapist. It took some time for him to achieve certain exercises unaided, a test of his strength and independence. To begin or end our session Steven was given a verse written specially for him, calling on all the qualities in-herent in him and which the Bothmer gymnastics therapy was trying to release.

## Music therapy

Music therapy is an art and science which has been practised in the Schools since 1948. In collaboration with Karl König, Susanne Müller Wiedemann (eurythmist, musician and curative teacher) worked out music therapies for children who are wholly or partially deaf and for children who have severe contact disturbances. Since then music therapy sessions for individual children have taken place regularly at our Schools. The therapy has been further developed in collaboration with doctors and therapists, both here and in other Camphill centres as well as the wider Rudolf Steiner Movement.

Music therapy sessions usually take place three times a week for a term or longer. For individual treatment the child is taken from his class to a specially prepared therapy room for a session which usually lasts ten to fifteen minutes. According to the individually designed therapy he listens to music, plays an instrument or moves to the music, played by one or more therapists using different instruments. The foremost instrument used is the lyre, designed and first built in the 1920's by Lothar Gartner, in collaboration with the composer Edmund Pracht, both of whom were early pioneers in anthroposophical work. It was designed to enhance the quality and stimulate the activity of listening, and its gentle, yet very clear tone is suitable for the most intimate setting as well as for a large hall. It is pleasurable to even the most highly sensitive children, and some high or low notes can be perceived by many deaf children who often have islands of hearing. Depending on the particular need of a child for whom the therapy is designed, various other instruments such as recorders, wind and string instruments, and a wide range of percussion instruments might also be used. They are chosen because of their different tonal qualities which are due to their specific overtones. Melodies, intervals, single tones, pitch, harmony, rhythm and metre are elements used therapeutically to work deeply into the living process of specific organs and can aid Ego–integration of a growing individual, as well as work on the emotional life. Composing and designing such a therapy requires relevant medical and musical knowledge as well as therapeutic and artistic skills and, therefore, it needs the close collaboration between doctors and music therapists. The music is always produced live by the therapist(s); recorded music, tapes or radios are never used.

Music treatment can also be given to groups of children suffering from similar types of impairment, such as deafness, partial hearing, aphasia, hyperkinesia and maladjustment. A different programme has been worked out for each of these groups and sessions take place daily, preferably at the beginning of a school morning. Often a coloured curtain or screen across the window sheds a coloured light into the room which adds to the effect of the therapy; for example, red light tends to stimulate limb and metabolic functions and soul activity, whereas children bathed in blue light, which gently reduces the flow of blood through the brain, are "cooled" and calmed. This treatment can also bring healing or, at least, relief, stimulation and comfort, to children and young people who may suffer from severe autism or psychosis. It can open up ways of communication which are otherwise barred for those who cannot naturally respond to the spoken word and consequently do not adequately develop speech. Another example of the help that can be given was observed when a severely anorexic young girl had music therapy, especially designed for her: after two terms she gained normal weight.

## "Listening space" therapy

Nowadays, all of us are exposed to overstimulation of and attacks on our senses, especially on our sight and our hearing. Particularly city dwellers are subjected to the noise of traffic and the press of crowds rushing about. Most shops have recorded background music which is either very loud or quietly plays on our feelings, lulling us into a false sense of security. Our eyes are confronted by the movement of crowds and traffic; and huge, often flashing advertisements, all declare that their goods are the best. Most of us watch the television and this medium, regardless of the content of its programmes, adversely affects our vision, our concentration, our ability to communicate with each other, and it can make us restless. Our imagination may be dulled (or even distorted as is the case with children who become obsessed with certain images). The amount of violence or sexuality seen on television may awaken destructive, untamed tendencies in those who watch it. These effects can be witnessed in our breathing. Long hours of television viewing produces shallow breathing; a sudden loud noise such as a motor cycle engine may take our breath away. All children are sensitive to excess sensory stimulation and children who have handicaps are especially vulnerable.

The "listening space" therapy was devised by Susanne Müller Wiedemann and others. It is carried out daily by our music department and benefits many of our pupils, particularly those who are hyperactive and, therefore, cannot concentrate effectively. It may also be beneficial for children who suffer from an aphasia and it is especially important for those whose breathing lacks depth and rhythm.

Before the therapy a group of three or four children waits in a room near the hall where the treatment is to take place. Each child is then accompanied into the hall by an adult. The musicians: a lyre player, a choroi–flute and recorder player are ready waiting in the hall, out of sight of the children. They sit at the back of the hall behind the children. The curtains are drawn, giving a warm, dim light. The principle of this therapy, as with most therapeutic activities, is to start where the child *is,* and slowly lead him to an experience which the therapist wishes to bring to him. So here we start by taking up the restlessness and continuous activity of the child and then slowly leading him to an experience of peace, permeated by the quality of listening. The music played initially is composed of short swift notes and the child is encouraged to take many short quick steps forwards in time to the music. This corresponds to what he knows so well: hurrying forward into the world. Then for a short time, long, slow notes are played and the child is helped to take slow steps backwards, the music coming from behind him. Then again the fast music comes with the hurrying forward. Gradually the long slow notes and the slow steps backwards increase in duration and the fast music diminishes, thus bringing the child to rest, to an experience of peace and the possibility of being quiet and listening.

In the second part of the therapy the child sits, listening to the music played to him from behind. He is now at peace and able to listen without having to be active or restless. The children are then lead quietly to their classrooms where, instead of being restless and lacking in concentration, they are able to sit peacefully and listen to their teacher.


## Curative eurythmy

In eurythmy, employed as curative exercise, the movements are developed so as to make them still more powerful in their effect on inner mental, as well as organic processes. There curative eurythmy exercises can be used, particularly when an inner response is lacking or some inner process is too weak or one-sided in development. Curative eurythmy is a specialized study in itself and the particular movements to be used in each case must be prescribed by a patient's doctor.

Curative eurythmy movements arise out of the sounds of speech: on the one hand the consonants and on the other the vowels. The forming quality of the consonants can be recognized in organic nature: the rolling "R," the enveloping "B," the ebbing and flowing of "L" and so on. The vowels are the expression of our inner attitude and mood. We say "Ah" in wonder, or "Oo" when we feel chilled. A little child will open its arms to the world in "Ah," we cross our arms in "Eh" as we grow older, shutting out the world and achieving self-consciousness. With "I" we become upright.

Man learns to stand upright within the forces that work from the Earth. These are centrifugal forces. From the periphery come centripetal forces: they are active not in heaviness, but in buoyancy; we become aware of them by their effect on the fluids of the body, in the circulation and the functions of the organs. In curative eurythmy we use the inflowing forces in the consonants, where there is a disturbance of *form*, for example, in arthritis or paralysis. We work with the vowel movements where the *function* or the organ is disturbed. The curative eurythmist should mediate between the irregular movements of a sick organism and the ideal healthy movement. She should move as perfectly as possible, so that the movement can work on the ill–adjusted movement of the patient. The growing number of patients suffering from movement disorders shows how important this is.

Since its inception in the 1920's the practice of curative eurythmy has grown considerably. Several hundreds of curative eurythmists have been trained and are active in a range of schools, including those which offer special care. They also work in adult clinics and in private practice, always in association with a doctor. Remarkable results have been achieved and new ways of healing discovered.

## Painting therapy

The understanding and use of colour and form in painting has been recognized as an important aid to the work carried out in the Camphill Schools. Painting therapy is given on either an individual or a small group or class basis, the former being more therapeutic, the latter arising through the adaptation of the class work, with individual attention being given to pupils by the teacher. We use methods based on studies undertaken by Rudolf Steiner and further developed by artists, therapists and teachers.

It is our experience that guided painting therapy, where emphasis is placed on achieving balance and harmony of colour and form and healthy, graceful movements, helps many children towards an experience of overcoming certain limitations. This form of painting therapy improves the rhythm and depth of breathing, increases alertness and calms the restless child. Its foundation arises out of an involvement with, and understanding of colours and their relationships. Out of this, and the study of many children's pictures, the therapist develops his feeling and understanding for the various ways children relate to and use colours and the many forms and compositions that arise. The rainbow colours, the natural environment, Man, animals, plants, the landscape and seasonal changes form a basis of inspiration for the exercises. The child uses the primary colours only and achieves the full spectrum of rainbow colours through the interaction between these. The use of the rainbow colours is particularly important as they have a pure, uncomplicated quality arising out of the meeting of light and darkness, as can be seen when looking through a prism.

On commencing painting therapy, a child is initially encouraged to paint a few free pictures; sometimes a theme will have to be suggested. Out of careful observation of the way the child tackles the picture, his use of colour, general movement and handling of the brush, the therapist can create an exercise to help the child overcome principle hindrances that manifest in the picture and his general behaviour. The tasks given depend on the age, capability and concentration of the child. For a young child an exercise may involve painting one or two colours. The forms might simply arise out of the meeting of colours, for example, yellow and blue meeting to form green, or green can become the green hills arising between the light and air (yellow) and the water and earth (blue). No exercise is approached intellectually or analytically. We appeal to the child's or young person's "feeling" judgment. We ask him to "feel" into the hills, the wind, the rocks, the trees and of course, the colours themselves. Themes for painting are often chosen from nature, not to be naturalistic but in order to see its relation of one form and colour to another giving a harmonious quality which then can reflect back on the child and build up a greater sense of wholeness. A technique we have developed to help the younger pupils towards these experiences of living colour is to soak the paper in water, then lay it on a board and finally wipe off the surface water with a sponge, leaving the paper damp.

It is helpful to look at the pictures with children at the end of the painting period. When painting trees, in a group for example, the individual trees appear very different, some showing thicker trunks, others no roots, yet others lots of scattered branches and leaves. By comparing his efforts with those of others, the child has an opportunity to achieve a more balanced sense of form on the next attempt.

*Veil painting* is a technique of stretching the paper by soaking it, wiping off the surface water with a sponge, taping the paper to a board, allowing the paper to dry and then applying layers or veils of water colour, building up the colour steadily by allowing it to dry between each veil or wash of colour. This is a very disciplined and calming technique suitable for young people from thirteen upwards. The layering technique can be applied with greater depth and imagination with the sixteen–year-old by painting in broad veils of thin colour, developing form out of sweeping spaces of colour. How one veil passes over another in relation

*Exploring colour in therapeutic painting*

to the rest of the veils of colour in the composition becomes very important, giving a deep sense of freedom and beauty as one masters the technique in which there are no outward illustrative props to hold on to.

Painting therapy applied in this way can lead children and young people to develop through coming to terms with colour and form. They can thereby compensate for any one-sidedness imposed on them by their handicap.

A child suffering from deprivation and maladjustment, who seeks perfection because he is afraid of making mistakes, gains help and encouragement in exercising his imagination and learning to "play" with colour; a child with epilepsy, often caught in dark, over-rich colours and cramped forms, can be led, with help, to the experience of a well-proportioned plant with uncramped leaves; a child who is restless and overexcited can come to peace when painting a tree that has roots in the ground, a firm trunk, and branches that are not stretching into infinite distance; a child withdrawn or psychotic, who hides within severe patterns of colour, can be led to experience the "social" delight of intermingling of colour.

## Riding therapy

Riding as therapy is well known throughout the country and our own approach has been developed since the late 1970's. The Schools have a small but well-designed indoor riding school for four to five fully trained horses. The therapy, prescribed in our clinics, can be helpful for a broad spectrum of our pupils: those who are autistically withdrawn, have difficulty in establishing their breathing rhythm and might even withhold speech, those who suffer from epilepsy and not least young people who have behaviour problems and may have suffered childhood deprivation. It is helpful in instilling self-confidence, improving powers of concentration, balance and co-ordination — and, not least, it provides joy and a sense of satisfaction. The therapists are curative educators who know our pupils and share life with them in our community.

Horse riding therapy has a certain relationship to music therapy and sometimes we use both in successive blocks. The horse walks at a 4/4 rhythm, trots at a 2/2 rhythm and canters at a 3/4 rhythm. In broad terms these movements can be experienced as relating to music as follows: walk to rhythm, trot to harmony and canter to melody. Most of our children can learn to trot. Securely guided by the therapist, they feel enveloped in the warmth of the horse and increasingly are given the experience of mastering the horse independently. The rhythm of the horse naturally helps regulate the rhythm of the child's breathing. The movement harmonizes breathing and heart beat, can be a satisfying and reassuring experience and thus support the flow of speech. The canter is of specific therapeutic value for children and young people who tend to be too tense and might have convulsions. The horse is the only animal which increases its grace of movement when carrying a rider and in cantering, lifts the rider out of gravity in rhythmically repeating movements. The experience of this rhythm can work deeply into the emotional and even organic processes of a young person and help him to achieve a better balance between gravity and levity, relaxation and concentration. The canter is also suitably used for adolescents who feel slightly overpowered by the growing heaviness and density of their own body. In our experience few of our pupils can learn to guide the horse in a good walking rhythm. This requires the rider to direct his awareness from the head, downwards through the spinal column, right into the tips of the toes and the ability to urge the horse on to walk in a forward–going manner. It calls for a good "Ego–control" and calmly directed will.

The therapy sessions last for twenty minutes to half an hour and are usually taken in blocks of six months, two to three times a week. To begin with, children are taught to approach the horse gently and learn to groom it while the therapist "talks" to horse and rider to instil confidence in both. Gentle grooming leads on to stroking and putting the face against the body of the horse, taking in its warmth, its softness and its smell. The horse is fitted with a purpose–designed broad roller with two large leather handles. It has various points for fixing the reins, because the positioning of the horse's head is essential for the therapy. It allows the child the direct contact of riding bareback and not yet having to hold the bridle.

The therapist then helps the child to mount and holds the horse on a lunge. When mounted the pupil leans forward, strokes the animal's mane and neck and reaches out to its ears until he feels confident. He then proceeds to ride without further aids which, of course, requires that the horse is trained to a high standard. The therapist instructs the voice-trained horse to walk and gradually widen the distance until he can stand in the centre of the arena and guide it to walk in a fifteen metre circle.

Next follow further confidence–building exercises, such as freeing the hands from the roller, performing rhythmical arm movements while the horse is standing, then in motion. Catching and throwing bean bags and balls of different size and weight is a further step, progressing to catching and throwing a two foot copper rod. The pupil is then introduced to different trotting speeds and this helps to establish a good breathing rhythm. Then, especially with adolescents, the 3/4 canter might be used. Eventually the lunge can be disconnected and while the therapist can still control the horse with his voice, the pupil increasingly gains the experience of mastering the horse by himself. In the last part it is brought to "stand" and the pupil lies back on it, lets his arms hang down and closes his eyes. Horse and rider stand quietly for two to three minutes in complete relaxation. Finally the rider dismounts, pats the horse and leads it back to a corner of the arena to be tied up.

For older pupils who have developed sufficient riding skills, saddle and eventually stirrups can be introduced. Attention is paid to precise handling rather than speed. As the young person learns to guide the horse with confidence he is helped to gain control of his own emotional life. Teaching of riding skills might not be appropriate for all young children but it can support the harmonious development of adolescents. The experience of the age old relationship between horse and Man, overcoming fear and learning to guide a highly sensitive and loved animal is, in itself, a moral training. It provides much joy and simultaneously is a fine indicator of the young person's development in self-control, confidence and maturity. In addition the care of the animals, grooming, feeding, cleaning stables and tack, is a good discipline. Many of our older pupils experienced this as a "privileged job" which taught them to improve their skills and become reliable.

## Play therapy

Play therapy as practised here is an important aspect of our therapeutic work with children suffering from various handicaps. It reaches with dynamic force into the depth of the child's inner life and can open up realms which otherwise remain in the subconscious. The child can be led from a set, inflexible way of being into a future with new possibilities of expression and experience. It is a therapy aimed at the child who is in need of liberation from the "prison" of his own personality.

The play therapist is requested to work consciously on her own self

*Discovering the world through play*

so that she can create an inner space in which the child with all his inappropriate pent–up emotions, mixed up concepts, bizarre habits and confused memories can be encompassed. Anthroposophy can give guidance for such a training in which receptivity and tranquillity, openness of mind and clear thinking, active involvement and positive objectivity are fostered in the therapist and made available to the child. The curative educator, and particularly the therapist, need to be aware that their own habits influence the "life space" of the child. The environment they create builds "a nest" which may work directly on the physical organism of the child, influencing his wellbeing. By working on her own emotions and actions the therapist helps harmonize the child's breathing and rhythm of sleeping and waking. She will support the child in developing new habits of living and being, which are no longer continuously inter–rupted by bizarre behaviour and restlessness. It is the task of the therapist to bring harmony into the inner life of the child. In trying to achieve this the genius of language and true communication can help her to find the right word at the right time thus creating order where formerly was chaos. In her endeavour to perceive the wholeness of the child the thera–pist is guided and permeated by an ideal image of Man and she can thus bring healing to the child in need of special care.

Play therapy is conducted individually and depends entirely on the needs the therapist recognizes in a particular child. Without judgment and in quiet acceptance, the child is received both in the playroom and in the therapist's "inner space." She has to be willing to absorb and bear with the child's affliction without rejection or fear. She can allow herself to be moved but not overwhelmed. Though accepting, the therapist is not totally permissive. She is careful not to unleash unbridled aggression or destructiveness but uses her skill to lead these, should they arise, into creativity. Play therapy is most effective, if it can be carried out in daily sessions of about forty–five minutes for a period of six to eight weeks. Through such a relatively short period, the intense therapy can work into the whole organism of the child and help transform his ill or even patho–logical trends of behaviour. Such a period allows the child to gain secur–ity first of all in the play therapy session and then gradually in himself. The next steps of new ways of being are a gradual integration into daily social life, and having the ability to gain more benefit from education and school work together with others in the classroom.

The following example illustrates the development of a child who needed a much longer period of play therapy, because of the severity of his disturbances. Ben was a severely disturbed child, filled with fears, fixed to routine, obsessed by rotating objects and driven into such despair that he felt compelled to smash his head violently against any wall, table or door. On first coming to the playroom, he was filled with suspicion but soon the room became a place of refuge. At that time Ben was unable to play, for bizarre shreds of thoughts popped up continuously in his mind driving him relentlessly to destruction. Any noise made him jump: for weeks, the passing of the dustbin lorry posed a threat, the crunching up of things, the destruction of anything whether imagined, material or alive, haunted him and caused violent outbursts. Gradually, Ben became responsive and instead of his confused and bizarre talk, he began to verbalize his upsets. He accepted little changes in routine and environment, coped with small restrictions, such as taking a little less paint. He could ward off the "upsetting" rattle of the dustbin lorry by producing a "counter–noise" with the tambourine. Remarkable progress was followed by spells of setback. Periods of dramatic outpouring of emotional tension gave way to times of withdrawal. Obsessions were transformed and "transferred" through manifold means of reflecting: by playing and acting, drawing and painting, as well as verbalization. In the course of time, Ben learned to look at himself in amazement and puzzlement. He discovered and learned to accept that he too is changing and that to be alive means change, development and continuous transformation. The painful process of his self–recognition is incomplete and will have to be accompanied and supported in many ways and for a long time.

## Therapeutic drama and role play

The aim of this therapy is to develop a free dramatic encounter which fosters a young person's skills in communication and self–expression. It helps to reduce inner tension and pent–up emotions and can strengthen the growing individuality. It is suitable for adolescents who have out-grown the stage of play therapy and is mostly conducted individually although it can also be suitable for therapeutic work with groups. As a rule, sessions of approximately one hour take place weekly. They can be in different locations which offer a variety of possibilities for acting, such as a small sitting room, a large hall, a classroom or a bedroom, and these can alternate as required. The therapist begins the first session in utmost peace but with no preconceived ideas or special plans. She tries to be open and receptive to everything that the young person presents. Sometimes it helps to break the ice and create the potential for an intimate situation by sharing morning break or afternoon tea, but this should not become a habit. The therapist may sit at a table but close to the young person using a letter file with his name on it in which she can, with his help, make notes, record the sessions and include drawings, paintings or any illustrations he may wish to add. The awareness of this record has a special therapeutic value for the young person. It is explained that it is up to his initiative to find ideas, words and develop a play. There is joy in the making up of his own play: anything can happen. He is free to choose any part — man, woman, child, animal, plant, machine and their interaction. The following example may illustrate the development of sessions.

George, fifteen years old, tall, dark haired, had at the age of thirteen, stopped speaking except when playing with small children. His communication consisted of grimaces, pulling and twisting his wide open mouth from side to side, sometimes producing inarticulate sounds or incomprehensible whispers. It seemed that a dialogue with him was impossible. After some time spent with patient coaxing and encouragement, George wrote, in large clumsy letters, the following suggestions for a "play":

HenmRE, HNNvAVH, ANReheANhen

He drew a small scribble, reminiscent of a circle, in one corner of the sheet of paper. The therapist realized that the circle represented a byre on his father's farm, and the letters, three of his bovine friends — Henry, Hannah and Ann. Soon a square of chairs in a corner of the hall became the byre and George, as the farmer, tried to drive the cows out into the field. The therapist, acting as Henry, Hannah or Ann waited to be called out but these cows were hard of hearing. After some fruitless attempts, farmer George's speech became so commanding that the cows, one after the other could not help but obey. At the end of the "day," Ann, the cow, refused to leave the green pasture and George, the farmer, shouted at her furiously: "Come on!" and drove her back into the byre. In the next session they exchanged parts, George, acting the cows, joyfully portrayed the character of each one in an astonishing performance of differentiated cattle–moods.

*Therapeutic drama with an aphasic group*

In the third session both therapist and George had become good friends with the cows and George introduced a new element: fire broke out in the stables. A telephone conversation, purely imaginative without props, was acted in great urgency. The therapist, at the other end of the large hall, as fire officer on duty, did not rush out the fire brigade until every word of the message that George the farmer conveyed was clearly understood. At last the fire engine arrived and George was the busiest and most effective fireman, of course, leading Ann, Henry and Hannah to safety.

In the fourth session the cows changed to horses which were struck by lightning. Again there was a prolonged telephone conversation with the vet, portrayed by the therapist, who eventually arrived by helicopter. The farmer gave detailed instructions where the vet should land and how he should treat the horses. In the course of the further sessions George volunteered more and more "necessary" words in emergency situations which he had invented: a bull had run away; he was pursuing a burglar; he was a shopkeeper who had to describe to a blind lady customer, everything he had in stock. A year later when George left school and returned home to his parents' farm, the family were happy that he could now converse again with the adults at home (albeit still grimacing). The drama sessions had opened up new possibilities of verbal communication which they could now extend also at home, with further practice.

The "exciting" stories, invented by the children and young people themselves, open the first door of verbal communication but are of value only as starters for more subtle sketches. It is the task of the therapist to guide her pupils not only to express rudimentary emotions such as shouting and swearing after an "accident," but to strengthen and maintain their feeling and perception for human situations and develop a true dialogue. The latter may be rudimentary or may lead into human depth with the most subtle use of words, depending on the severity of the impairment the young person has to cope with. It takes some time before the abilities gained in an intimate therapeutic session can also be used in daily life, but when it is achieved the young person can progress in developing towards maturity and will be aware of his achievements.

## Speech therapy

The ability of a child to communicate with others, expressing himself verbally and intelligibly is one of the foremost human achievements. In recent years speech therapy has widened its scope from correcting faulty pronunciation to enhancing communication skills. With many pupils in our Schools it is helpful also to work with movement and gesture which in child development precede speech. Learning to speak in the second year of a child's life is preceded in the first year by achieving uprightness and walking, which require a fair degree of motor control. Speech development is intrinsically dependent on a refined mastery of voluntary movement, not only of the speech organs, but of the whole motor system. Hence any failure of harmonious movement development directly influences the development of speech. The child's manner of walking: heavy, hurrying, irregular, hesitant, is reflected in his flow of speech. Good co-ordination, gesture and finger movements are a basis for the child to develop free speech. The larynx itself can be looked upon as the most refined muscle, comprising on a small scale not only the whole variety of, but also the finest possible human movement. Speech therapy in the Schools takes this movement aspect into account and comprises a wide variety of therapeutic approaches. Therefore, we distinguish between auxiliary therapies and speech therapy itself. The former can precede or accompany the latter and may include horse riding, eurythmy, trampoline, rhythmical exercises (clapping, walking, stamping), the pentathlon (the five classical Greek gymnastic exercises) in a simplified form and other, often individually designed, movement exercises. All these auxiliary therapies help the development of an adequate awareness of the body schemata and of the three spatial dimensions. They are directed to the movement and rhythmical aspects underlying speech.

In speech therapy itself three different approaches are used:

1. Exercises to train the muscles and awareness of the instruments of speech, especially lips and tongue. These pre-speech exercises are indicated for children with facial paresis and those who never went through the initial baby stages of sucking, blowing and babbling.
2. Orthodox speech therapy, concentrating on proper enunciation and correction of faulty positioning of lips and tongue, as well as building up a useful vocabulary.

3. The majority of children require an approach whereby the basic enhancement of movement skill is now combined with the actual use of the spoken word.

The following can indicate some of the lines along which individual therapy sessions are designed:

Children with abundant, yet unintelligible language learn to order their sentences by carefully stepping out the syllables, first mechanically, then bringing in the natural flow of speech.

Children with lack of concentration walk or clap rhythms of poems which are chosen for their enlivening or calming effect (rising or falling rhythms).

Children who speak monotonously are helped to gesture the meaning of what they want to express.

Children who are inhibited, or where speech seems to be locked up in the speech organ, benefit from throwing a cushion whilst speaking.

All children needing articulation exercises find pleasure and encouragement when speaking is accompanied by throwing a ball or weighted scarf. The joy of moving can help the child over the hurdle of his embarrassment at having a speech problem. Speech sessions are usually concluded by listening to a well spoken poem.

## Spinning and weaving

We use a broad range of crafts to aid education and therapy, among them spinning and weaving. Pupils who attend our weaving studio on a daily basis are over fourteen years of age. Initially they learn to tease, card and spin the wool, which are the first stages of the whole process. These activities require increasing concentration and directed application but have a soothing effect and engender the peaceful atmosphere which can be sensed by anyone who enters the weaving studio. For spinning, the traditional spinning wheel is used which requires the development of a particular skill and co-ordination between hand, foot and eye. It is always a special joy for a new trainee pupil to achieve and master the ability of operating the spinning wheel. He is then ready to start weaving.

Two types of looms are used: the upright loom, also called the rug-loom and the foot powered floor-loom. The former has an ancient tradition and can be helpful as a first stage of weaving, particularly for those young people who still have severe difficulties with concentration and co-ordination. Working in the upright plane rather than in the horizontal, allows them to participate more directly in the process of creating a pattern. Working with the foot-power shuttle loom is another step requiring a different kind of awareness. The hands are left free to throw and catch the shuttle and to beat the weft. The feet in co-ordination with the hands can use four pedals in many different sequences to create the most beautiful patterns.

The pupil is guided to work with increasingly complex patterns which require increasing strength of concentration and a rhythmic interplay between hands, feet and eyes. Woollen and silk threads are used and many of the threads have been dyed with plant dyes made in our studio. It is a great joy for a young person and gives him a sense of achievement when he discovers the length and beauty of the cloth he has created. He sees that the finished articles are used for many purposes and are held in high esteem by those who receive them. In our experience not only outer material is woven at the loom, but through the activity of weaving, the young person simultaneously builds up an inner fabric, an inner sense of creation, of self-worth, an inner tapestry of morality.

## Work as therapy

Amongst the older pupils in Camphill are some severely handicapped youngsters who benefit from work as therapy rather than as a preparation for employment or apprenticeship. These young people, who may have physical as well as mental handicaps, need to experience the dignity and meaning of responsible adult work even though they might never be able to fulfil all it demands. In our experience it has been of great benefit to them simply to witness an adult at work, particularly when participation, at least initially, might not have been possible or was severely limited. The learning of some practical skills may have come as an added benefit, but they have been primarily helped to develop a sense of responsibility and have an experience of dignity; the latter not being necessarily dependent upon the former. It is important for a young person who cannot do a day's work that the situation is accepted for what it is — no more and no less. If he experiences that his individual worth is recognized his inabilities will not seem demeaning. Therefore also, he is not paid a wage as this would be both unrealistic and condescending, although as he is growing, his need for having his own money is accepted.

The progress and development of one young man, Duncan, is typical of such individually created situations. Duncan suffered from spastic quadriplegia. Although he was mobile, he was not confident when walking over rough ground. He was also severely retarded and had no speech, communicating with a few basic gestures and five or six Makaton signs. After due consideration he was placed with a gardener in one of our estates, although he had no relevant skills in this area — he could not handle any of the tools or push a wheelbarrow. At fifteen he was still very dependent upon being taken to his classroom, helped on with his coat, told to wash his hands,and showed no initiative to do anything in his free time. The arrangement was that he would meet the gardener halfway through the morning, after an hour and a half in class, and accompany her in her work. At first he needed to be sent by his teacher and invariably came with his coat unfastened and without his wellington boots. A certain amount of time was spent helping him to learn skills and for the rest of the time Duncan watched and participated according to his ability. Over the course of the year fairly dramatic changes came about in Duncan. He was eager to start work and arrived appropriately dressed; he felt responsible for the gardens and demonstrated this, for example, by picking up stones on the lawn — regardless of whether he was "working" or not — or by informing the gardener of children stealing plums or of broken glass in the greenhouse. He felt motivated to learn relevant skills and put a great deal of effort and concentration into doing so, overcoming his physical disabilities to the extent of learning to push a wheelbarrow and use a bow–saw. Above all he was proud to return home at the end of the morning, being aware of the respect he had earned as a responsible person.

# Special therapeutic classes

The following gives two examples of special therapeutic classes which are created as need arises for pupils who for varying reasons cannot, for part of their school life, participate in our curative education mainstream classes.

## *The aphasic class*

The aphasic class provides a highly specialized programme of visually and practically presented lesson contents and therapeutic exercises for those children with primary difficulties in word understanding and speech. The pupils all have additional handicaps, often including autistic or psychotic tendencies, being a developmental reaction secondary to their inability to understand words or even gestures. Children aged ten and above may join the group from other classes where the spoken word is increasingly relied upon to convey an essential part of the syllabus. At that stage and even more so as they approach puberty, these children experience an intolerable frustration when they cannot grasp the content of their lessons and may react with severe outbursts of violence.

The following is a description of a typical morning's school of an "aphasic class" with six to eight pupils, however, the sequence and details may change according to the needs of the pupils.

They begin with lively movement together, using rhythmical stepping, throwing and catching or expressive gestures to draw the children into a group activity, as they frequently relate only to the teacher. The class then follows a well–established routine of hearing a morning song and spoken verse, changing the calendar, noting the day's weather and so on. During this, the pupils can relax into the familiar routine, with even those who are hyperactive learning to stay in their places and settling behind their own desks. The teacher draws these often restless children with their individual obsessive concerns into an attentive but relaxed mood of listening, focused on the teacher to begin with. Each child is frequently called upon in some way; one may be able to say some words of the verse, another might copy the date onto the blackboard or accompany the song with a chime bar. Each one does some exercise he is working at over several weeks — learning to clap rhythms or to hum a single melody perhaps. Basic skills are practised daily in this way whilst establishing a rhythm of participating before the class and then observing quietly whilst others take a turn — the type of social skills normally needed in conversation. This first part of school is an important daily opportunity to share a form of conversation which is otherwise a major loss to the aphasic child.

When the mood is right, the day's lesson content can be presented. Because of the age differences in the class, our syllabus cannot be followed in the same way as in other classes, although the small numbers make it possible to give each child's work a particular emphasis appropriate to his age.

A general subject for several weeks work may be to follow the making of bread from harvesting, threshing and grinding to eating the loaves they bake. In doing this, there is opportunity for practical activity, painting, acting–out related stories and many other non–verbal ways of learning. A trip to the local bakery can be used to lead the older pupils into handling money and even to the understanding of working and earning. Each step may need many repetitions to allow a child to follow what is happening. As many of the basic concepts and connections which make the world intelligible are unknown to these children, it is important that this process of basic learning is taken as far as possible.

At each stage the teacher emphasises a few key words, whenever possible teaching children to speak, write and recognize them. Returning to these words days or weeks later can show whether a well–known word has been forgotten or has become established in the child's vocabulary. The pupils show very different and specific difficulties; some become apparent only over a long period of observation but can then allow significant help to be given. For example, Gary, a bright and willing older boy with very limited word comprehension, was found to consistently confuse a few specific sounds. Therapeutic help with special eurythmy exercises could then be concentrated on this problem.

The general lesson to the whole class takes thirty to forty minutes. Development of particular aspects is taken up later in the morning when the teacher and his assistants work with smaller groups. After this the daily movement therapy takes place, allowing the class to be active together again and making a refreshing break from the classroom.

All the pupils show some abnormality in their movement, ranging from the over-tense and cramped to the flaccid, with some having a physical disability. The movement exercises fall into two general areas: — gymnastics aimed at developing the ability to pronounce words (executive speech), and special eurythmy, aimed at the understanding of speech.

In the gymnastic exercises children learn to run, jump, aim and throw, and to wrestle. Doing this, the tense pupil can be encouraged to let himself go in running and leaping, the more flaccid has to try to push an opponent out of a circle or onto the ground. Such exercises can help those children who need to be taught how to form the sounds of speech and to give flow and clarity to their speaking. The movement of throw-ing at a target can lead on to blowing out a candle and later to saying the sound "f." Having the range of large gymnastic movements is a great help when working at the finer movements of speaking and is a respite from the frustrations of stumbling over the spoken word.

During eurythmy lessons the aphasic class move together in expressing a wide range of moods to appropriate music: angry (stamping); slow, sorrowful (walking); exciting chases and merry (skipping). These pieces bring colour and variety into their emotional life, as these children are often bound to the routine and objects they see around them. Leading dramatic music into expressive gesture is a first step towards trying to communicate for some. Without the wish to express themselves, learning sign languages such as Makaton or struggling to say a few words is of limited value. When the desire to communicate is strong enough, many non–speaking children can convey very clearly what they want to tell. One very withdrawn boy led his teacher to a picture of a school bus and, by pointing to himself and miming sleeping, he expressed eloquently that he felt unwell and wanted to go home to bed!

Understanding the spoken word requires that the hearer can respond to the activity of the speaker, recreating in himself the movements of the other. When this resonance does not occur, language is only a flow of more or less musical sounds and does not take on meaning — as when listening to a foreign tongue. In the eurythmy lessons the children learn and practise movements and gestures of the arms which correspond to the movements of the mouth and larynx when speaking. By imitating this "visible speaking" when hearing speech they can begin to develop an appropriate response to the activity of the speaker and make words meaningful and distinct from other sounds. Once a child suffering from aphasia begins to recognize words and realize that they can convey meaning, his emotional life and mental activity go through a profound change and he can relate to others as well as to himself in a new mean-ingful way. To achieve this is a central and most important aspect of our aphasic treatment.

The movement therapy is followed by breaktime and the many indivi-dual needs for instruction and therapy are fitted into the next hour. At the end of the morning the class gather briefly for a third time of moving together before dispersing to the various family groups.

Experience has shown that children suffering from aphasia become in-creasingly frustrated as they reach adolescence unless their word understanding has improved. It makes a great difference to their personality development if they can appreciate what the spoken word is and have at least a small vocabulary. It is a great help and joy to them if they can follow the content of their lessons with understanding, even if they cannot reproduce it in spoken words. It opens up the meaningfulness of the world, which is otherwise closed to them. As adolescents they can then become more contented and participate with other pupils in our Upper School and further education courses.

## Special therapeutic group

The special group creates a setting for children who cannot, as yet, adjust to one of our "mainstream" classes and have great difficulty of integrating into any social context. It is a small setting allowing for an intensive, therapeutic and individual approach. Most of these children suffer from diverse multiple handicaps, motivational failure and severe withdrawal. They have a short concentration span and their word and concept understanding is severely impaired.

Their school morning consists basically of three parts. The first part begins with exercises to stimulate self–awareness and interpersonal contact, awareness of the day of the week and the season. Then the lesson proceeds with basic work to stimulate understanding and the forming of simple concepts involving a chosen topic which, as far as possible, would relate to the curriculum appropriate to the age groups involved. Social awareness is fostered through movement exercises which call for interpersonal contact such as moving in an expanding and contracting circle, giving and receiving a copper rod to the rhythm of a hexameter or other rhythms. Each day of the week and each season of the year is emphasised visually through drawing and painting, through singing and music performed by the teacher and involving the pupils. For some children music and art are the only gateway for communication open to them. Often dramatized seasonal stories are used.

The whole class is "bathed" in beautiful language through listening to a brief presentation of poetry. This enhances their relationship to the essentially human qualities of language and speech. Speech exercises are practised individually as appropriate. The experience of rhythm in music and poetry is emphasised by walking to the beat of a chime bar or tambourine.

Also in this class the daily presentation of a school subject repeated over several weeks is an attempt to rouse the pupils' interest in the world, as otherwise they tend to be preoccupied with their own body, with certain obsessions or they seem to be devoid of interest. Subjects are chosen to enrich their experience and, even if only partially, build up their personal awareness and relationship to a wholeness of the image of Man. Movement, acting, painting, drawing and modelling are used to present a few concepts so that they can be grasped and remembered. Here again language and music are used and enhanced through movement which rouses joy in the pupils. Through these means certain inner experiences and qualities can be evoked such as being filled with fear and then the courageous overcoming of fear; being sad or joyful; and the I/you relationship.

In the afternoons the pupils of the special therapeutic group have block periods of arts and crafts just as most of the other pupils do, but they need a special approach with extra guidance and help. These include painting, modelling (often relating to the subjects studied in the morning), handwork and basic skills such as the use of scissors, tying a bow with cords and laces, doing up buttons, threading beads, basic weaving, also co–ordination and matching exercises, walking and drawing forms. A special session is devoted to mixing and kneading dough and then baking bread. Some pupils attend a therapeutic gardening group.

Most of these pupils find a sense of security in their group and are keen to be included. Nevertheless, their motivation often remains distant and therefore they can hardly work independently. They do respond, even if in a limited way. Their pace of learning is slow and often interrupted by their restlessness and oversensitivity to their environment. Some of them make enough progress so that they can benefit from joining one of our "mainstream" classes corresponding to their age group. Some learn to participate in practical work as they grow older but the majority need an intensive therapeutic setting for many years.

# 8 Towards the future

## The school leaver

On leaving school as young people we go from a sheltered place, designed by adults who wanted to help us grow up and learn what they thought would be appropriate to enable us to make our way in life. We have as yet little life experience and, therefore, our healthy hopes about our future are often built up on illusions and beautiful fantasies. At first we expect a new freedom in a wide sea of possibilities though eventually it narrows down to a journey against the current between the banks of earthly realities. We then have to meet a challenge of transforming our treasured feeling of freedom into an inner quality which can accept destiny and develop social warmth.

For young people who have mental, physical and/or social handicaps this transition can be much more difficult than for their better endowed contemporaries: a precarious time when they may swing between fantasies and feelings of hopelessness or between maladjusted behaviour and apathy. Nevertheless, the majority of our adolescents try to make more effort than their contemporaries. They come to terms with their "handicap" which severely narrows down any choice in training and career, and restricts their social life.

We try to offer our school leavers time for further education, work experience and social maturation and they fully participate in the discussions about their future. Any further education and training here or elsewhere are indicated only when they request and agree to it. Our young people are often not verbal or coherent enough to express a definite view. Much confidence and patience are needed before their views can come to expression.

It can happen that we are unable to contain a pupil because of increasingly violent behaviour and have to discharge him though he might have wished to stay on. Outbursts of violence may be brought on by an underlying epileptic condition or a feeling of severe deprivation and having an uncertain family background. In these circumstances the human capacity of our staff is tested; we may have a sense of failure when we can see the good in a young person and yet cannot, in our setting, prevent him from doing harm, for we do not have secure accommodation.

In recent years local authorities have widely recognized the need for extended schooling and have provided the necessary funding. The majority of our school leavers wish to continue their education, as can be seen from the appended (1990) list of thirty–eight school leavers. Most were aged between sixteen and twenty–one and ten had completed our extended schooling or further training. They progressed to the following:

| | | |
|---|---|---|
| 23 | (60%) | Further training (not at our Schools) |
| 2 | (5%) | Sheltered employment |
| 1 | (3%) | Gainful employment |
| 5 | (13%) | Unemployed |
| 4 | (11%) | Transferred to other schools |
| 3 | (8%) | Not known |

Of these:

| | | |
|---|---|---|
| 14 | (37%) | went to live at home. |
| 11 | (29%) | live in hostels |
| 7 | (18%) | are at other Camphill Communities for Further Training. |
| 4 | (11%) | were transferred to other schools. |
| 2 | (5%) | had to be hospitalized. |

This survey gives a picture typical of the last decade, and it is helpful when trying to evaluate the achievements by pupils and staff through years of intimate sharing and working together.

The transition from work and life in schools or centres for further training to sheltered village communities or work in the open society requires a change of attitude for those who have handicaps as well as the so–called non–handicapped. In our Schools we seek to educate and effect change in our pupils which in turn requires the support of self–education by the adults involved. As educators we have to diagnose the hindrances in a child's Ego–integration — a term which will be explained below — both with regard to his body and his social environment. However, this kind of educational diagnosis should not be applied after school and training have come to an end. Some of our former pupils will, in due course, find their way to one or other of our village communities. There, life and work are shared together and life itself provides a schooling of self–education and the acceptance of an adult's "handicap" on the same basis as we would accept rain or sunshine. This approach calls for empathy which permits us to recognize another person's shortcomings within our own selves. With this awareness, individuals living in these communities — whether or not they have an overt handicap — can share friendship and a rich social life.

# Ego–integration

Ego–integration is the term we use to characterize the process of the spiritual individual entering through conception and birth into his body and the environment of family and nature, of folk and historic time. His body, with its organic functions, neurological system and senses, should become his "home" in space and time on Earth. Once he has begun to walk and talk, his Ego develops self–awareness which we call Ego–consciousness. Based on this he becomes a self–aware person who can remember from day to day and unfold his own motivation and morality. These evolve through interaction with his environment and take a long time to mature. In the early years of life the individuality expresses itself and radiates largely through bodily features and childhood play. During adolescence individual aptitudes and intellectual skills become apparent. Subsequently the young person is once more thrown into turmoil, feeling as if naked and unprotected, when consciously having to meet his own destiny. At this stage Ego–integration becomes an active struggle bet–ween world and self, reality and ideas. Ideals and ideas originate in our spiritual existence before birth and want to surface in the mind of the young person. They may clash with the values which are held by parents, peers and others. The joys and pains, indulgences and disappointments present a daily task of weighing up conflicting personal priorities. Such conflicts can cause anxiety and bring danger but are needed to achieve a healthy state of Ego–integration. Who in our time can as yet achieve it completely? The awareness of our imperfections in body, soul and spirit is an ever humbling experience which can lead us to realize that the encounter with a "handicap" in ourselves and in others has a deeper meaning: it should guide us as individuals and society on the way of becoming more fully human.

The following may illustrate what is meant here. One summer holiday in the mid–80's, four former pupils, all in their twenties, visited us. The first two were of superior intelligence but had been socially complicated and difficult youngsters. Marcus had completed a training as a shipwright and was now studying medicine. He had become a remarkably warm-hearted person and while here on holiday used his practical skills to carry out several repairs. Shortly after his visit we received a message that he had died in an accident. This was shattering news but his parents and we felt that his personal destiny was not without fulfilment and he might have achieved much of what he had intended in this life. James came for an afternoon. He was busy writing his doctorate in sciences. After having shown our premises to his wife, who had come along, he told us that he was not liked at the university but they could not throw him out because he had passed all his examinations. If he could not become a lecturer then he wished to become a tax inspector.

Of the other two, Edward made good progress while he was at our Schools as a boy, so his educational psychologist thought he could go to an ordinary school. Now he had become a drop–out, unsettled and un-happy, defying those who tried to help him and offer him a place to live. He was not in the habit of washing himself; one really had to air the room after he had left. A few years later we heard that he was conten-tedly living in one of the northern Scottish Isles. The local community there has an extraordinary way of being tolerant, taking him in and yet leaving him free. The fourth, Mike, was a little younger than the others. We had not been able to offer him further education and training because of his unpredictable violent outbursts. Probably they were connected with his athetotic movement disturbance and his background of childhood deprivation. He came to express his warmth and gratitude to some of our staff. A little later we heard he had felt that another man was making sexual approaches to him, and had overreacted. The result was that he was in prison serving a life sentence. Certainly these four are uncommon among our former pupils but their dramatic stories highlight the quest of Ego–integration.

Most of our former pupils are fortunate enough to live for a time at home or in sheltered accommodation. Some will eventually join an adult community of the Camphill Village Trust, or similar organization. There they integrate, are involved in useful work and can lead a life with much social contact and a wealth of cultural activity. Others prefer to live on their own in the open society where they usually lead what is actually an unintegrated and lonely life. They can be incorporated, but their handicap often prevents them from finding friends or any social life.

The following letter from a parent tells us about a former pupil who has found shelter and warm support at home and in his local community:

John was born in October, 1958. His birth weight was below 4 lbs. Three days after birth he had a convulsion, but he appeared to progress normally until at sixteen months he had a bad fit. From that time, it became increasingly evident that he was handicapped, both physically and mentally. His behaviour was difficult: he would scream if he did not get his way. He did not attack other children, probably because his co–ordination was so poor, but he was destructive: a visit to the supermarket could be a nightmare. By the time he was of school age, he could walk and talk sufficiently to make himself understood. He could take himself to the toilet and manage most of his dressing; although, to this day, he cannot fasten buttons at his collar and cuff. He went to a primary school in Edinburgh, where we lived at that time. He was disruptive and was sent to a special day school.

His brother, Arthur, was born in 1962 and his sister, Bridie, in 1966. Both developed normally. John seemed to welcome both his brother and his sister but on one occasion we were concerned that when John had been near his brother's cot, the baby had been scratched with no apparent cause. As Arthur grew up, his play was continually disrupted by John. It became impossible for the family to have a holiday together. John's grandmother, to whom he was particularly attached, looked after him sometimes so that we could have a break. Arthur was showing symptoms of withdrawal and hence we were concerned at John's disruptive effect on the family.

John went to Camphill School, Aberdeen in 1970. One thing we were able to do was to have a seaside holiday with his brother and sister. On his first holiday, we were struck by John's calmer behaviour. This improvement continued although it took several years to achieve a satisfactory result. There were a number of relapses. We were able to resume taking family holidays together during John's summer holidays. In his final two years at Camphill, by which time we had moved to London, John was able to travel between London and Aberdeen by air, unaccompanied, at half term.

John left Camphill in 1975. He now attends the local adult training centre. He was able to adapt to life within a busy family and he is regarded with affection by the local community. We take him on holiday at home and abroad and to social functions. Two years ago, he enjoyed a cycling holiday in Germany with his father. His brother and sister have been successful in their education and careers and their friends have accepted John.

We are sure that the coherence we have enjoyed as a family is a direct result of the work which Camphill did for John. Without it, there may well have been three handicapped children and two demented adults. In particular, John's absence during term time enabled us to attend to the needs of our other two children; together, we were able to welcome John back for his holidays and integrate him into the family. Our one regret is that John did not go to Camphill a few years earlier.

NN
Parent


This fine letter speaks of John's difficulties and victories and does not mention the despair experienced by his parents and teachers alike when in adolescence he was, for a time, frighteningly aggressive. It is good fortune to have a supportive and loving family who can instil confidence in their youngster and even help the community to overcome severe hurdles.

# Achievements and aims

Curative education has its spiritual roots in the work of great pioneers of the eighteenth and nineteenth centuries such as Itard, Pestalozzi and Barnardo. The foundation for the work as we now know it, was laid in 1924 by Rudolf Steiner when he gave his Course in Curative Education.[14] It was attended by a small group of young educators and doctors who then initiated what became the worldwide movement of anthroposophical curative education. In 1940 Karl König, together with his youth group, mainly medical students and artists, who came as refugees from Vienna to the north–east of Scotland, founded the first Camphill Community. Now after fifty years of work in community life with children, young people and adults who have handicaps, we feel that we are still pioneering, for there is so much to learn and do better. Although there is a sharp drop in the birth rate in industrialized countries, the number of those who have handicaps remains significant. There is, indeed, a new tolerance in modern societies which allows some mainstream schools to absorb pupils who need special education. Nonetheless there is a continuing stream of children and adolescents who cannot cope in modern society and need curative education in an all round healing, educational environment.

Now at the beginning of the 1990's when a mother can choose to abort the child she carries because it might have a handicap, we meet a whole range of new handicaps: conditions caused by newly discovered viral infections or as yet inexplicable illnesses; increasing allergies to foods and environmental substances, or having some unknown causes; self abuse such as head–banging, aggression or severely disturbed sleep patterns; and there is also a still increasing stream of childhood deprivation. Scientific knowledge about the physiological and subtle chemical processes in the human organism has made magnificent progress. Yet we still know little about the embodiment of the human spirit. We have discovered much about the eye and the ear but we still do not fully understand how we see, hear and remember. Research and training in the field of curative education and its allied disciplines therefore must continue. So much more is yet to be discovered and as we learn more, our methods in therapy, teaching and care can offer better help where help is needed.

Another aspect is the social development of human community. "The child we love and about whom we despair" (as Thomas Weihs expressed it) can lead the way in teaching us about human development and society. (Also the adults who have a handicap can guide us to build true community life with them both in urban and country areas.) Every child embodies hope for the future. The child with a handicap then calls forth the best in the parent and in all those who want to uphold this hope. Here the Camphill Communities see an ongoing task.

The tradition of the Camphill Movement worldwide has established that it is possible to work out of love and not for the sake of a salary. It requires that we see the reason for our work in those who need it and that we can apply ourselves out of inner freedom. The words "love" and "freedom" have been debased in our time and therefore, it is difficult to use them with clarity. Where there is love we can act out of freedom but in as much as we feel fettered by material or emotional pressures, we are not free; and where we are not free, love is diminished. Yet forgiveness can kindle inner freedom even under very adverse outer conditions. The small yet precious light of freedom can be nurtured by our friends who live with handicaps, adults and especially children. They can give us daily lessons in the essence of love and forgiveness. They can teach us to develop mutuality in learning to live positively with handicap and illness. We must recognize our need in answering their need.

Social research and learning about human qualities are of a different nature than natural scientific endeavours. They involve us on a more personal level. We surely feel that freedom is a treasured part of "self" and we try to give it protection. One way is to try and secure it by taking out all kinds of insurances. Another way has been suggested by Rudolf Steiner at the beginning of the century when he wrote about the "Fundamental Social Law" referred to in Chapter 2 (see page 46)[15] An individual's wellbeing and freedom can be protected when his personal needs are met by what others provide. The proceeds of his own labour can then be made available to the others. In the course of five decades the Camphill Communities have shown that this can be a very practical fruit of the union of love and freedom. The developing social forms of our communities are yet imperfect and limited but we believe and trust that they will continue to widen and offer growing support to human society in the future.

This stands in contrast to many considerations of present day governments. They tend to be preoccupied with teachers' salaries and pupils' examinations. Rudolf Steiner held that examinations make a person restless and nervous, thereby reducing his true potential to learn and to offer a good contribution in life. In Camphill we have no examinations. Instead we aim to conduct assessments which support and strengthen the best qualities in pupils and teachers. They must therefore be based on confidence in the teachers — not on statistical averages. The cultivation of such confidence is one of the most important community endeavours. Living communities can support such endeavours when they are imbued by a spirit which unites individuals who live and work together and share in the joy and sadness which life has in store for them. In our present day society we shall depend for a long time on the safeguards of rules and regulations but they can only be based on past experience. Love and freedom are primal creative powers bearing within them the good for the future. The spirit of Camphill strives locally and worldwide to span situations arising from the past and human spiritual impulses which are of the future and need to be prepared for now. This spirit allows love and freedom to be effective in the present.

# Appendix

The following extracts are taken from: *Curative Education. The Course at The Camphill–Rudolf Steiner–Schools, Aberdeen.* This booklet was originally published in 1981 for the Faculty of Curative Education on behalf of the Association of Camphill Communities by Aberdeen University Press. It is currently (1992) out of print, pending revision of a number of details concerning hours of formal instruction and training.

The Course in Curative Education is conducted over three years and provides simultaneously the facilities for living and working with handicapped children. Theoretical and art courses and supervision of practical work take place at the Schools. Theoretical instruction and practical experience, train the student for independent and responsible work in curative education, which comprises the triad of:

*(a)* care and home life;

*(b)* teaching and special education and teaching based on the Waldorf School curriculum;

*(c)* introduction to and application of specialized therapies.

In the Camphill Course this triad of curative education is embedded in a fourth discipline: community living as a continuous path of learning. The Course offers the additional options of an introductory foundation year and postgraduate studies, in conjunction with other Camphill Centres and with colleges and universities.

Students who wish to serve the task outlined, need to acquire generic as well as specialized knowledge and skills, as described in a later section on the curriculum. In addition, and of equal importance to these, they are required to develop social and artistic creativity and inner resourcefulness. As a foundation for this, they have to accomplish three basic phases of development.

In the first year a sense of awe and wonder, with which all philosophy started, is fostered in the student. By learning to observe clearly the disorders of human physical and mental development, the student is helped to see the essential image of Man. The recognition of the image of Man is a guide to discerning each individual's personal ideal and to recognizing how one falls short of it. Everyone wishes to become more loving and clever, more enduring and skilful, yet it happens all too often that children — and older people — experience frustrations and give up their striving. As students learn to recognize this ideal in each child — and in fellow students and teachers — they become equipped to counterbalance the shortcomings and frailties of others within a social structure.

In the second year the students learn to strengthen their empathy and compassion. As individuals, they try to experience the other human being within themselves, to feel and perceive his frailties as well as his highest human aims, his darkness as well as the divine spark in him. In this process the students cannot but meet their own frailties too. The child with handicaps is a great educator in this respect. Through this contact, the students learn that the child can only make progress to the same extent to which the teacher is prepared to work on his or her own self-development.

In the third year a twofold process takes place. On the one hand the students broaden their awareness beyond the immediate house community, sharing in the responsibilities, for example, of the celebration of seasonal festivals with plays and pageants, and the administration concerned with finance and house management. On the other hand students have to acquaint themselves with specific therapeutic techniques and with the creation of therapies for individual children or groups. This approach may intervene deeply in the life and destiny of children and therefore requires conviction guided by the conscience of the curative teacher.

One of the students described her experience of this development in a nutshell by saying: "In the first year, you meet the child and this absorbs all your strength. In the second year, you begin to meet yourself; and in the third year, you try to widen your initiative and sense of responsibility over the whole community, and there you meet your limits."

In conclusion the following may be said about the course offered. The child who has a physical, mental or social handicap can be experienced, not as a disaster, but as an individual with a mission. He teaches us to develop conscience, empathy and a sense of wonder. His destiny, his being "different," helps his teachers, his parents and all those who are involved in his destiny, to develop qualities and attitudes which are so eminently needed if humankind is not to destroy itself and our globe. One of these attitudes is to unite clear knowledge with compassion and with the will to do what is good.

The members of the Faculty of the Course in Curative Education are responsible for the conduct of the Course as a whole and are personal tutors who accompany individual students through their training. The international structure of the Camphill courses in curative education is carried by an International Faculty, on which one of the lecturers of the faculty at Aberdeen serves as an executive.

Together with the members of the faculty, the staff of the Schools' community at Camphill take an active and responsible part in teaching and guiding students who live and work with them. These staff members are houseparents who are responsible for a family unit, class teachers, art and craft teachers and therapists.

Thereby, the Course is an intrinsic part of the striving and development of the whole community, a stimulus for research and enquiry, new approaches and reflection, added experience and fresh thinking.

By the completion of the Course, students should be capable of taking up one or more of the three fields of work described below:

(i) Responsibility in the home life and care of a small unit. This comprises care for the wellbeing and harmonious life of adults and pupils; correspondence with parents and authorities; preparation and celebration of seasonal festivals and adjusting life according to season and weather; catering and seeing that household needs are covered and met; simple home–nursing; ascertaining that remedies and drugs are regularly administered; ensuring that pupils attend school, special lessons, therapeutic sessions; attending to repairs and maintenance and many other regular and incidental activities.

(ii) Teaching a special class for children with varying handicaps. This requires having a working knowledge of the Waldorf School Curriculum and of the needs of a child at a particular age; the capacity to apply appropriate therapeutic approaches to children with reading, writing, co–ordination, concentration and dominance disabilities among others; a knowledge of the need to learn skills in meaningful lessons which will prepare the child for life in the open community.

(iii) Comprehension of the range of therapies (having gained experience in at least one of them) and knowing which of these should be recommended for a particular child.

The Course aims to ensure that having acquired these competencies the student should therefore be enabled to:

Give advice and guidance to untrained helpers.
Be in charge of groups of handicapped and/or disturbed children in homes, special units or classes.
Recognize and supply the need for mental and emotional stimulation, as well as enliven or calm children according to need, thus helping them to find their place in the community.

The Course is open to students from the age of eighteen years, though preferably older, as the Course calls on the students' readiness to mature.

Previous work experience or an initial professional training are desirable. Application is by letter and, where practicable, followed by interview.

Acceptance to the Course is based on the following qualities in the candidate:

Personal adaptability, and willingness to commit one's self to the needs of the handicapped child.

Willingness to live and care for a group of children with handicaps, in a family situation, and to learn from this experience to understand the human being, his development and his handicaps.

The ability to establish rapport with the children.

Preparedness to experience community life as a task in self–training and in social skills.

The intellectual capacity to follow the Course.

The faculty decides on the candidate's provisional acceptance to the Course. This decision is reviewed by the student, the student's tutor and house–parents at the end of the first half year. At that time, if his or her suitability for work with children and grasp of course studies are evident, the student will be accepted.

Throughout the three years the students evaluate their progress together with tutors and other senior members of staff, individually or in groups. The tutor keeps a record of work produced by each student, which includes written–up notes of courses, lectures and seminars; essays on specific theoretical courses; précis on set readings; diaries and progress reports on pupils written in co–operation with houseparents and teachers.

At the end of each year the student, members of the faculty and all who have worked with the student, assess his or her progress more formally and, together, decide on further studies and whether the student should go on to the following year of the Course. The tutors participate in the daily life of the Schools as well as in the Course and they are, therefore, in a position to base their assessment of the student's progress on their direct observation.

Special emphasis in the assessment of the student's progress is laid on the following:

Can the student apply acquired theoretical knowledge in the daily life and work with the children? Knowledge should become a source of empathy and social skills and not a mere accumulation of definition and theory. Practical ability and rapport with the children are vital criteria, as is the ability to work together with other adults.

In the final year the student is required to write and deliver a thesis giving evidence of independent research in curative education.

Students are awarded the diploma when the Faculty, in consultation with those who have worked closely with them, consider that they have success–

fully completed the Course. The final assessment includes an "Evaluation" stating in which field the student has shown particular gifts or application and which areas would require further effort. The award of the diploma may be deferred until an omission in the student's experience is rectified.

The completion of the Course and award of the Diploma is the occasion for formal celebration by all who have participated. Some students continue to a post–diploma year to establish proficiency and/or to specialize in home life, care and guidance, curriculum and special teaching or in a specific therapy.

# Notes and references

*(See bibliography on page 181 for full details of sources.)*

1. Pietzner, Cornelius (Ed.) *A Candle on the Hill,* page 26.
2. See Hailey, Michael. *Camphill Communities,* page 15.
3. Asperger, H. *Heilpädagogik,* page 1.
4. König, Karl. "Sinn und Wert heilpädagogischer Arbeit" in *Die Drei,* May 1974, page 229.
5. Rudolf Steiner's collected works are published by the Rudolf Steiner Verlag, Switzerland, and will when completed comprise over four hundred volumes: the first part containing fifty books including many collected essays and letters; the second over four thousand lectures. Steiner always spoke freely without a written text and, therefore, the lectures were being published on the basis of shorthand and sometimes longhand notes taken down as he spoke. He usually did not have the time to edit them himself. The third part is reproductions of his artistic work and photographs of his architecture and sculptures. English translations are available through the Rudolf Steiner Press, London and the Anthroposophic Press, New York.
6. Quoted from unpublished notes for Thomas Weihs' last public address at Ochil Tower, Auchterarder.
7. Loukes, H. *Teenage Religion,* page 62.
8. See Weihs, Thomas. *Embryogenesis,* pages 51ff and pages 75ff. See also: Schad, W. *Die Vorgeburtlichkeit des Menschen,* pages 7ff.
9. See König, Karl. *The First Three Years of the Child,* page 3.
10. Steiner, R. *Anthroposophy and the Social Question,* page 24.
11. Heydebrand, C. von *The Curriculum of the First Waldorf School,* page 1.
12. Harwood, A.C. "The Main Lesson," in *Child and Man Extracts,* published by Steiner Schools Fellowship, 1975, page 198.
13. See Raffe, Harwood, Lundgren. *Eurythmy and the Impulse of Dance,* pages 14f.
14. See Steiner, R. *Curative Education.*
15. See note 10.

# Bibliography

Asperger, H. *Heilpädagogik.* Springer, Vienna 1956.

Bott, V. *Anthroposophical Medicine — An Extension of the Art of Healing.* Rudolf Steiner Press, London 1982.

Bühler, W. *Living with your Body.* Rudolf Steiner Press, London 1982.

Davy, John, *Hope, Evolution and Change.* Selected essays. Hawthorn Press, Stroud 1985.

Edmunds, F. *Rudolf Steiner Education — The Waldorf School.* Rudolf Steiner Press, London 1987.

Emmichoven, F.W. Zeylmans van, *The Anthroposophical Understanding of the Soul.* Anthroposophic Press, New York 1982.

Glas, N. *Conception, birth and early childhood.* Anthroposophic Press, New York 1983.

Hailey, Michael (and Editorial Group) *Camphill Communities — Social Renewal through Community Living.* Association of Camphill Communities, Aberdeen 1988. (Obtainable from Camphill Bookshop).

Harwood, A.C. *The Recovery of Man in Childhood — A Study in the Educational work of Rudolf Steiner.* Anthroposophic Press, New York 1982.

—— *The Way of a Child.* Rudolf Steiner Press, London 1988.

Heydebrand, C. von, *Childhood.* Rudolf Steiner Press, London 1988.

—— *The Curriculum of the First Waldorf School (with a supplement on English language and literature).* Translation and additional notes by Eileen Hutchins. Steiner Schools Fellowship, Forest Row 1989.

Holtzapfel, W. *Children's Illnesses.* Mercury Press, New York 1989.

—— *Children's Destinies.* Mercury Press, New York 1989.

König, Karl, *Being Human (Diagnosis in Curative Education).* Anthroposophic Press, New York, and Camphill Press, Yorkshire 1989.

—— *The First Three Years of the Child.* Floris Books, Edinburgh 1984.

—— *In Need of Special Understanding.* Camphill Press, Yorkshire 1986.

—— *The Human Soul.* Floris Books, Edinburgh 1986.

Lievegoed, D. *Phases of Childhood.* Floris Books, Edinburgh 1987.

—— *Phases, Crisis and Development in the Individual.* Rudolf Steiner Press, London 1985.

Loukes, Harold, *Teenage Religion.* SCM Press, London 1962.

McAllan, Audrey, *The Extra Lesson, Exercises in Movement, Drawing and Painting.* The Robinswood Press, Stourbridge, revised edition 1991.

Meyer, Rudolf, *The Wisdom of Fairy Tales.* Floris Books, Edinburgh, and Anthroposophic Press, New York 1988.

Pietzner, Carlo, *Questions of Destiny, Mental Retardation and Curative Education.* Anthroposophic Press, New York 1988.

—— *Who was Kaspar Hauser? — An essay and a Play.* Floris Books, Edinburgh 1983

Pietzner, Cornelius (Ed.) *A Candle on the Hill — Images of Camphill Life.* Floris Books, Edinburgh, and Anthroposophical Press, New York 1990.

Raffe, M., Harwood, A.C. and Lundgren, M. *Eurythmy and the Impulse of Dance.* Rudolf Steiner Press, London 1974.

Schad, Wolfgang, *Die Vorgeburtlichkeit des Menschen (Der Entwicklungs-gedanke in der Embryologie).* Urachhaus, Stuttgart 1982.

Steiner, Rudolf, *Anthroposophy and the Social Question — Three Essays.* Mercury Press, New York 1982.

—— *Curative Education — Twelve Lectures.* Rudolf Steiner Press, London 1972.

—— *The Education of the Child.* Rudolf Steiner Press, London 1981.

—— *The Study of Man.* Rudolf Steiner Press, London 1990.

Taylor, Miss M.J. (Convenor) *Learning Together.* (Issues in designing a school curriculum for pupils with severe mental handicap). Scottish Curriculum Development Service (Edinburgh Centre) 1984.

Treichler, Rudolf, *Soul Ways ( The Developing Soul–Life Phases, Thresholds and Biography).* Hawthorn Press, Stroud 1989.

Warnock, Mrs H.M. (Chair) *Special Educational Needs.* (Report of the Committee of Enquiry into the Education of Handicapped Children and Young People.) HMSO 1978.

Weihs, Thomas, *Children in Need of Special Care.* Souvenir Press 1988.

—— *Embryogenesis in Myth and Science.* Floris Books, Edinburgh 1986.

—— "Love and Despair." In: *Perspectives on Policy and Practice in Special Care.* Edited by Charles Hills, Georg Schad and Steve Baron. Proceedings of the first Thomas Weihs Memorial Seminar 1984. Department of Education, University of Stirling; Association of Camphill Communities 1986.

Weihs, Anke, *Whither from Aulis.* A Childhood Autobiography. Floris Books, Edinburgh 1989.

zur Linden, W. *A Child is Born.* Rudolf Steiner Press, London 1985.

## Current Periodicals

*Curative Education and Social Therapy*. English edition. Quarterly, edited by Johannes Denger. Konferenz for Curative Education and Social Therapy, Dornach, Switzerland.

*Camphill Correspondence*. Monthly, edited by Deborah Hudson. Camphill Village, Botton, Yorkshire.

*Child and Man*. (Education as an Art). Biannual, edited by Brien Masters. Steiner Schools Fellowship, Forest Row, Sussex.

*The Golden Blade*. Edited by William Forward and Andrew Wolpert. Floris Books, Edinburgh.

# Index